LEAD UPWARDS

SARAH E. BROWN

LEAD UPWARDS

HOW STARTUP JOINERS CAN IMPACT NEW VENTURES, BUILD AMAZING CAREERS, AND INSPIRE GREAT TEAMS

WILEY

Published by John Wiley & Sons, Inc., Hoboken, New Jersey.
Published simultaneously in Canada.

For general information on our other products and services or for technical support, please contact our Customer Care Department within the United States at (800) 762-2974, outside the United States at (317) 572-3993 or fax (317) 572-4002.

Wiley also publishes its books in a variety of electronic formats. Some content that appears in print may not be available in electronic formats. For more information about Wiley products, visit our web site at www.wiley.com.

Library of Congress Cataloging-in-Publication Data is Available:

ISBN 9781119833352 (Hardback)
ISBN 9781119833376 (ePDF)
ISBN 9781119833369 (ePub)

Cover Design: PAUL MCCARTHY

SKY10033115_031122

Dedicated to Erin Rand, Colleen Blake, and Matt Harada, whose tremendous leadership examples, support, and friendship have profoundly impacted my career trajectory. Also, in memory of my late grandmother Zelda Lipman, who taught me the power of lifelong learning and unconditionally believing in people, including oneself.

CONTENTS

CONTENTS

CONTENTS

Introduction: Why Startup Leadership Matters at Every Level

So, why haven't you been an executive before? It looks like you were qualified years ago.

The venture capitalist's remarks were part of his due diligence in determining whether the early-stage startup he invested in should hire me for a marketing leadership role. But upon hearing his backhanded compliment, my heart sank. While I was grateful for his affirmation that I was qualified to be considered for the position we were discussing, it made me wonder: why *had* I waited when my resume suggested I had enough experience for a startup executive position years earlier?

Fast forward several years later, and I'm a vice president of marketing at an early-stage venture—a startup executive. That conversation with the VC was a wake-up call, motivating me to learn how to transition from mid-level manager to department leader, which I have done thanks in great part to the support of my executive coach, friends, my CEO, and peer network.

In hindsight, I didn't aspire to become a startup executive earlier in my career because I didn't know it was possible. I didn't understand what qualifications were required or which skill gaps I might need to address. I knew that there was a startup leadership tier I wasn't yet part of, but I didn't know how to reach it. I was also unable to picture myself as a startup executive, with so few role models in the industry who were like me, an openly LGBTQ+ woman. Lack of visibility does make a difference and can be a self-perpetuating cycle.

Although we've seen progress in recent years, the technology industry is still overwhelmingly homogeneous at the leadership level. At the time of publishing, nearly half of all startups don't have a single woman on their executive teams.[1] A 2019 study from the National Center for Women and Information Technology (NCWIT) shows that while women are about 60 percent of the total workforce in the US, they are only 25 percent in the computer technology industry.[2]

Within tech, people of color are fewer and egregiously rare in startup leadership. According to a study conducted by the Ascend Foundation, numbers of Black women in tech declined by 13 percent from 2003 to 2017.[3] According to Deloitte, approximately 2 percent of the tech workforce is Black, 3 percent is Latino or Latina.[4] Note: for a book specifically focused on the challenges women of color in tech face that includes fantastic resources; I highly recommend Susanne Tedrick's book *Women of Color in Tech: A Blueprint for Inspiring and Mentoring the Next Generation of Technology Innovators*.

The information technology industry is one of the crucial drivers of economic prosperity worldwide. It is a multi-trillion dollar industry.[5] In 2021, the global cloud computing market alone was worth $270 billion. The tremendous wealth and opportunity in technology have been unevenly distributed. Inclusivity at all levels of startups drives economic equality.

I didn't have a great response for the investor all those years ago, but if I could go back in time, I would share these statistics with him (and my younger self), about systemic challenges that historically have led to capable, qualified people from under-represented backgrounds being under-represented in startup leadership.

I would have also thanked him for inadvertently pushing me to see myself as the kind of startup leader I'd always wanted to be but didn't believe was possible.

Early in my career, I developed a passion for B2B SaaS and the cloud and its promise to provide tremendous value to businesses and users across the ecosystem. I've been a B2B SaaS marketer ever since. More than a decade later, I still love the space and feel grateful to be a part of it. At the time of publishing, I've had the privilege of being a marketing leader at five startups that have been sold for more than $300 million combined.

Along the way, I became interested in improving diversity and inclusion throughout our startup ecosystem. I founded an LGBTQ+ technology group called Flatirons Tech in Boulder, CO, which is part of the NCWIT Affinity Group Alliance and partners with startups and global technology companies like Google, Splunk, Twilio, Twitter, Workday, and other technology companies to increase tech inclusion across the Front Range and beyond. I've also become a mentor at Techstars, a global accelerator with more than $19 billion in market cap, and Backstage Capital, which funds and champions founders from under-represented backgrounds. Both organizations aim to increase inclusion within the startup landscape. I've discovered a calling supporting joiners from under-represented backgrounds, and helping us achieve our best careers and lives possible within the startup ecosystem.

The startup road isn't easy. A startup career can be rewarding, but navigating it can be challenging and confusing, as few resources exist to help startup employees advance. Unlike established companies, startups are disrupting markets or creating new ones, and career trajectories are often nonlinear. Startup employees must forge their own paths.

As they grow and mature, startups are expected to behave more like enterprises, and this presents a challenge and an opportunity for rising leaders. How do you scale your own leadership to meet the demands of the market, including customers and shareholders, as your company grows?

There were more than 12 million tech employees in the US in 2019[6] and more than 800,000 technology startups operating in the US alone in 2020.[7] Most startup resources focus on helping founders and chief executive officers succeed. But for every CEO at a startup, there are *multiple* executives charged with leading and scaling the company's departments. Forbes reports that Leadership Development is a $366 billion industry, yet surprisingly few resources aim directly at helping startup executives succeed in their roles, which can be challenging and with high turnover. According to industry group Pavilion, the average tenure for a startup revenue executive is just 16 months.[8]

As the people who oversee making and selling products that are forging our future, CEOs and founders aren't the only ones making an impact. For every founder, there are many people who are "startup joiners," a term coined and popularized by venture capitalist and author Jeffrey Bussgang. Startup joiners have the power to shape their companies and the market. This book offers advice about being a top performer in a startup leadership role, whether you're already one, or are looking for your first executive-level job.

Perhaps you're a manager or director at a startup and would like to know how to transition into an executive role. I want to demystify what the role entails to do it well. I will also share the skills, experiences, deliverables, and presentations that a startup executive needs to know how to execute in order to be successful, including presenting at your first board meeting or creating an annual plan for your department and getting cross-functional stakeholder buy-in. You might already be a startup executive, and want more tips and advice for being successful at navigating an ever-changing startup environment.

This book includes real-world stories from leading executives, venture capitalists, and founders, alongside frameworks and practical guidance that executives outside the CEO role can benefit from. It shares clear frameworks for success, practical advice, in-the-trenches stories, and crucial guidance that will help current and aspiring startup leaders land and excel in their roles.

Doing well in this environment takes a special set of skills. This book describes how to navigate predictable, crucial executive areas, such as how to land your first executive role at a startup, succeed within your first 90 days on the job, how to manage relationships with your CEO, team, fellow executives, and board of investors. It also discusses how to scale your impact and role as your company grows, and navigate challenges and setbacks.

After reading this book, you'll have insights into the following questions:

- What is it really like to be a startup executive?
- How will I know if I have what it takes or even want to be a startup executive?

- What differentiates startup executive roles from management or other contributor roles, and what does it take to make the leap?
- How can I leverage my nonlinear path or under-represented background to become a startup leader?
- How do I manage my first 90 days in a startup executive role successfully?
- What does it take to effectively manage my team and myself in our remote, post-Covid world?
- How do I successfully communicate my results to our CEO or our board?
- How can I scale my impact with the company as the company grows?

While this book is not by any means exhaustive, it should help you make more sense of the world of tech startup leadership and make better decisions about your career along the way. I believe making the successful leap from startup manager or director to executive should be demystified to make the path more accessible and inclusive to the widest and most diverse range of talent. New employees look at the executive team to see if it is inclusive at the highest levels; this book specifically addresses barriers for under-represented leaders and how to overcome them.

Becoming an executive should be within reach of far more rising startup leaders. I hope to help empower the next generation of executives with tools to excel. For those who lead startup joiners, the founders and investors, this book provides tools for supporting, promoting, and fostering executive talent. Stronger leaders benefit our entire startup ecosystem. It's time that we focus on up-leveling the next generation of startup leaders, which this book aims to do through the inclusion of relevant case studies, examples, voices from startup leaders from diverse backgrounds, with tested, practical advice readers can put to use in their own careers on their journeys to "lead upwards." Let's get started!

PART I

BECOMING A STARTUP EXECUTIVE

CHAPTER ONE

What It's Really Like to Be an Executive at a Startup—and How It's Different from Being a Director or Manager

> *Is being a startup executive really that different from being a manager or director? Yes. But probably not in the ways you think.*

Prior to becoming a startup executive, my view into the role was limited. I saw how the "executives" behaved in our one-on-one meetings and while presenting to our entire company during all-hands meetings. I noticed how they emailed, messaged, and comported themselves at the office. I observed how they spoke in our companies' all-hands and how they behaved at holiday parties. I watched them, as most startup employees do their leaders. (If you're reading this, know that people are paying attention to your behavior.) But my view wasn't close to the full picture of what their roles demanded.

At various companies I'd worked for, many of the executives' calendars were fully booked in meetings so often I wondered how they got any work done. What were they *doing* during these blocks? Beyond their busyness, I wondered what that translated to in terms of what their jobs required on a day-to-day, weekly, or quarterly basis.

Now that I'm an executive, I understand that the bulk of work done by an executives team is challenging to grasp as an individual contributor or even mid-level manager. While there's been a movement to increase transparency across the startup ecosystem and more companies openly share their operating principles and salaries to their employees and even to the public, much of the inner workings of a startup leadership team are hard to see if you're not a part of it. This chapter covers what a startup executive role involves behind the scenes, including insights from executives on what their work-life entails on a daily, weekly, and monthly basis.

"The more senior you are, you execute less, and you have to be efficient with your time and need to empower your team to achieve your goals," says marketing executive Rachel Beisel. "You're in a lot of meetings because you're often the facilitator between departments and between employees in those departments."

The reason that executives spend so much time in meetings is that decision-making is their most important responsibility. While startup leaders will always execute to some degree at earlier-stage companies (including the founders and CEO), their ability to strategize and decide is *why* they exist at the company.

"As a founder, I have decision fatigue," said AQUAOSO CEO and co-founder Chris Peacock. "I expect my executives to constantly make good decisions in their areas, even in the absence of all of the data."

Executives are charged with managing managers, meaning their direct reports generally have their own reports. This "skip level" hierarchy requires executives to empower their reports to make good decisions and own *their* areas.

The level of hands-on work you do as an executive will vary based on your startup's stage and maturity. Early on in a startup, you'll be spending more time on execution, doing things like shipping a new landing page, or editing copy, or creating financial models. These deliverables are a big part of how your success is measured early on. But as your company grows, you'll need to delegate and manage other people who can do those things while you manage their productivity.

WHAT DOES A STARTUP EXECUTIVE REALLY DO?

Each week, executives spend the bulk of their time communicating with each other and their teams to align the strategy and programs with business goals. They collaborate across departments, incorporating new data to adjust the course as needed. Many startup executives who come from working at larger companies struggle with the balance of execution and strategy. You have to "zoom in and out" as executive coach and former Microsoft North America CFO John Rex calls it, and do execution as well as strategic work.

In addition to the general management of others and their team, a startup executive owns a department or "function" and its goals. A department is usually a team of teams and the overall strategy, vision, and goals that this person sets for their department must roll up to the overall business goals, which are translated to their team's sub-goals.

A STARTUP EXECUTIVE'S SCHEDULE: A WEEK IN THE LIFE, AT A GLANCE

A sample startup executive schedule:

Daily

- Checking dashboards to view metrics and results measured against quarterly and/or yearly goals.
- Providing feedback to campaigns or other work products of teams within your team, usually at key milestones—early to verify direction (e.g., this product roadmap change aligns to our strategy for the business/team) and "buy-off" at final stages of delivery (yes, this press release has my seal of approval for publication, and my job is on the line if we screw it up).
- Cross-functional meetings with other executives or departments.
- Reading up on the latest news in your market or industry vertical.
- CEO syncs and department team meetings.
- Checking in on project management updates from your team on Slack, Asana, or another communication tool.

Weekly

- 1:1 with your direct reports; ensuring your reports and *their* reports are succeeding, and the team is tracking to Objectives and Key Results (OKR); troubleshooting any issues; and tracking their career goals.
- Weekly updates cross-functionally to other teams and your CEO.
- Measuring progress against OKRs.
- Feedback and/or sign off on key projects in your department.

Monthly

- 1:1s with your direct reports; ensuring your reports and *their* reports are succeeding, and the team is tracking to OKRs; troubleshooting any issues.
- All-hands presentations to the entire company and/or business unit.
- Board updates.
- Updates to your CEO and/or cross-functional stakeholders.

Quarterly

- Reporting on a Quarterly Business Review (QBR) and/or Objectives and Key Results (OKRs).
- Evaluating strategic decisions weighing performance and/or new data.
- Board updates—deck, pre-read materials, and/or live presentation in a board meeting.
- Setting OKRs for the next quarter or half.

Annually

- Annual reviews and retrospectives, including reporting wins, failures, and what you've learned to your CEO, fellow executives, and the board.
- Annual planning, forecasting, headcount, and budgets.
- Financial models and planning—tracking CAC and LTV.
- Supporting fundraising efforts.
- Performance reviews for your teams and yourself (sometimes semi-annually).

Your daily, monthly, quarterly, and annual activities depend on the maturity of your department and company. Smaller startups may forgo annual planning and instead rely on quarterly planning cycles. You and your CEO may meet three times per week vs. once, so take the above with a grain of salt. Note: for more detail on running effective 1:1s with your CEO, team, and board, see the chapter on building relationships.

OTHER DIFFERENCES BETWEEN NON-EXECUTIVE AND EXECUTIVE ROLES

Accountability at the Highest Business Levels

Startup executives are accountable for delivering business results to company shareholders, including your co-founders, fellow executives, the board and investors (your founders' bosses), and other employees. As an executive, you have the most ownership (including, likely, equity) and accountability of anyone on your team. Unlike individual contributors or mid-level management, startup executives must build business strategies and execute them. Pavilion leader Jennifer Rice refers to the concept of building business opinions (vs. being an order taker) as "having a theory of business."

As a marketing executive I am expected to form and communicate data-driven opinions on how to generate demand within target accounts to increase my startup's market share and grow revenue. My CEO and cross-functional peers can help and my team will provide input, but, ultimately, I own and put my name on a plan. I need others to believe in the plan, but first I have to believe in it and champion it. When it succeeds or fails, I am the one who's responsible. No one will hand these plans to us to go execute as startup leaders as they did when we were mid-level managers (although great ideas can and do come from anyone on the team). It's on us to strategize and enable our teams to deliver results.

OWNING THE "WHY" OF THE WORK

As business leader Peter Drucker would say, there is a difference between doing the right work and work done right. Your job is to make sure that the programs, tactics, and tools your team uses roll up to the overall business goals of your organization. Own the "why" of the work—not just "should I run *this* PR campaign?" but "should we run *any* PR campaigns, and is that the best investment of our limited budget, and why?" This is how executives need to think. You'll constantly be making tradeoffs.

How will your department's strategy and tactics lead to the business achieving goals? What have you learned in previous quarters or even recent weeks and days that informs the work you're doing? These are the types of questions executives are expected to answer. Continuing to think through "why" is just as important as "how." The best startup leaders constantly learn to improve and achieve faster, better results.

DEPARTMENTAL UNDERSTANDING BEYOND ONE NARROW AREA

As an individual contributor or a manager of a small team, you can get away with having depth of expertise in one area without much breadth across the department. Your remit may be narrow. Being an executive comes with an expectation that you understand the fundamentals of many areas of your department, not just one specific area of functional expertise. This includes things like knowing about front-end engineering vs. full-stack, and how to manage multiple technical teams running multiple products, etc. While you aren't expected to know everything (that's what hiring your team is all about), you'll need to expand the breadth of your functional area expertise in order to hire, retain, and effectively manage a team of high performers who execute across your function.

RESPONSIBILITY FOR BUILDING AND LEADING A HIGH-PERFORMING TEAM

You can be a "team of one" as a "head of" at a startup for longer than you'd think. I did it for several quarters before hiring my team in a recent executive role. But you can't reach any kind of scale without growing your organization. If you can't hire a team, that can be a dealbreaker impediment to your success. First-time executives often fail to attract the best talent, because candidates may feel that their abilities as a leader are yet to be proven.

We'll dig into how first-time startup executives can succeed at hiring in later chapters, including how to build an inclusive, high-performing team that will support each other's success. If you want to be an executive (or already are one), be prepared to adopt a "servant leader" mindset and stretch your skills in effective management as one of your highest priorities.

SIMPLY PUT: IT'S A BIGGER COMMITMENT

Startup executive and Diversity and Inclusion (D&I) expert Aubrey Blanche says that while it's possible to live a balanced life as an executive, we shouldn't underplay the lifestyle impact. It really is a bigger commitment than a non-executive role.

"There is often discussion that you don't have to give up some of your life to be a leader. We do a disservice to people when we're not honest about the big life impact that comes with taking on leadership roles," says Blanche. "There certainly are unique situations where you can work part-time and be a VP, but it really does require you to put your job relatively central to your life. I think we should go into that choice with eyes wide open," says Blanche.

LESS COMPANIONSHIP AND CAMARADERIE WITH OTHER NON-EXECUTIVE STARTUP EMPLOYEES

While you'll enjoy camaraderie with your fellow executives, don't expect to be chummy with your team in the same way, especially if you were promoted from within the ranks. Being the team leader gives you power and a position of authority that won't allow you to act as you did before, even as a manager. That power is significant. You can't expect to be on "even footing" when you could fire, promote, or give pay rises to your people. Their livelihood is now tied to your decision-making, and that puts you in a position of power that shifts the dynamics within your relationships.

You're also dependent on your team. No startup executive would be successful if they didn't have a high-performing team rallied around them, but it's inherently imbalanced and skewed by authority dynamics. It's much harder for a report to get their boss fired than vice versa. If you fail, your team may stay on and you may see the door, but it wouldn't be them making that decision. Because of this power imbalance, you must act accordingly.

We must not abuse this power imbalance or put our direct reports in positions that could hurt them (for example, dating them, or engaging in behavior that's inappropriate for the hierarchy). Some startup executives have *too* much power over their teams and reports. Unlike at big companies, some startup leaders can get away with a lot without oversight, which is thankfully becoming less the norm thanks to movements to increase equity and inclusion and expose and enforce consequences for bad behavior. The checks and balances within the startup ecosystem have been lacking for too long. Thankfully, many startups are creating opportunities for employees to have a real voice in giving feedback on their managers and supporting a healthy, inclusive culture on teams.

Acknowledging inherent imbalances, we can still create strong, positive relationships with individuals on our teams. Even though we can't be peers while we're managing our reports, we can get to know them as individuals, help them be stewards of their own careers, give them growth opportunities, and support their contributions and productivity. We can do our best to treat everyone with the kindness and respect they deserve and ensure they have a psychologically safe and affirming work environment that honors their individual needs as well as the collective team needs.

If you're signing up for an executive role, embrace the fact that your ability to consistently perform these management responsibilities makes a true difference in people's lives. Aspire to do this well, knowing even with good intentions you can and will make plenty of mistakes along the way. We'll talk about how to deal with this later in the book in the section on team management.

EXECUTIVES HAVE THE MOST CONTEXT OF ANYONE IN THE DEPARTMENT

As an executive, in most situations, you'll have more context about the business than others on your team. I didn't realize how much this context impacted my team's decision-making until I became an executive. A full schedule of cross-functional meetings gave me a real-time understanding of the business that no one else on my team had. It was up to me to regularly communicate these to my team so they could be effective in their roles. It's an executive's job to communicate to their team what's going on outside a department to others. Due to the pace of startup life, this isn't always as expeditious as the speed at which they're garnering new intelligence. Some information can't be shared with the team due to confidentiality or other concerns.

This may sound simple, but it's a powerful concept. As a leader, you'll often know more than others on the team about any given topic. You have to somehow get everyone rowing in the same direction on a regular basis when they can't know all of what you know right away.

While you can't share everything with every team member at all times, with your guidance you can steer your reports towards what they need to be successful in their roles. It helps to build trust so that they will follow you as you make decisions to which they don't have full visibility.

WHO'S QUALIFIED TO BE A STARTUP EXECUTIVE?

There is no minimum number of degrees nor years of experience required to be a startup executive. You read that correctly: None. There are 24-year-old CEOs of startups and there are 24-year-old VPs of sales at startups. Some startup executives have MBAs from fancy top-tier business schools and thirty years of business experience. Others didn't graduate from high school. Some don't become startup leaders until they've got two decades of business under their belts and some are promoted after five or six years of startup experience.

No lack of credentials should keep you from aspiring to become a startup executive. Will a twenty-six-year-old who's been working for four years be better suited to be a successful startup executive than someone with two or three times that amount of experience? It depends, just as it depends for founders. According to *Harvard Business Review*, the average startup founder is 45, even though stereotypes would have us believe it's much younger.[1]

Here's another stat from *Harvard Business Review* that motivated the inception of this book: women tend to only apply for jobs that they're 100% qualified for vs. men will apply when they only meet a selection of the criteria listed.[2]

Harvard Business School author and leadership coach Anne Morriss says that, based on her and her partner Frances Frei's research, demographics bear no weight on who succeeds in a leadership role.

"Our research shows there aren't major demographic differences in who ends up 'killing it' at a startup in a leadership role," says Morriss.

"Demographics do matter in who gets promoted, who receives the resources, and who has access to the networks," says Morriss. "But once you make it into a leadership role, the people who thrive are those who bring curiosity to their own strengths and weaknesses and the strengths and weaknesses of the individuals around them."

NO ONE IS TRULY QUALIFIED TO BE A STARTUP EXECUTIVE BEFORE THEY'VE DONE IT BEFORE

Another crucial point to let sink in: *no one* is fully qualified to be a startup executive until they've done it, because there are skills and job requirements you can't master until you've encountered them. This is true whether you're a "big company" person learning to map your skills to the startup arena or a mid-level manager or director aiming to "scale up" to mature with the business.

Unfortunately, in the past, many members of the dominant group in the startup industry have found a way around this fact by being promoted based on *potential*, which often translates to "looks like the guy who had the job previously." According to Kim Scott, executive coach and author of the bestselling business books *Radical Candor* and *Just Work*, "Men are more likely to be rewarded for perceived potential, whereas women get promoted purely based on past performance."[3]

So how do we help a broader group of people translate the skills and qualifications they have into a startup leadership role? We need to remove the bias of "qualification by association" and break the role down into objective, essential requirements.

WHAT QUALIFICATIONS AND SKILLS ARE ESSENTIAL ON THE JOB AS A STARTUP LEADER

Due to systemic and internalized bias, many qualified people never go for leadership roles in a startup, even if they want them. About ten years into my startup career, I noticed that many startup leaders had backgrounds that *looked* comparable to mine on paper before going for the executive role. I wondered what their resumes were missing that made them qualified.

It turned out that these individuals were not necessarily more qualified. Once in the roles, they'd learned the skills of the role, which was something I (and many others) were perfectly capable of doing too. If you're comparing your resume to someone else's, you may not see the work they've done or the mentorship they've received outside of their official roles. And, truth be told, many startup executives get their first "shot" based on perceived potential and learn the skills they need on the job. So let's unpack the skills and backgrounds that are necessary to become an effective startup leader.

Here's what you *do* need to make the leap from mid-level contributor to startup leader:

- **Valuable and measurable expertise and track record of success in a key startup functional area** (e.g., engineering, marketing, product, sales, customer success, operations).
- **Some experience in management.** If you're a first-time startup executive and first-time manager, it will be much harder.

- **Willingness to learn how to work with financial shareholders.** Until you've done a board meeting (we'll talk about how to prepare for these), you won't know what it's really like.
- **Willingness to learn how to communicate effectively at scale, with multiple stakeholders.** Make great slides and write clearly and persuasively.
- **Be data-driven.** All startups require data to inform their decisions, and today's startup executives are expected to develop data literacy.
- **Willingness to fail and improve.** Startups are built around learning and iterating. You'll need to do this constantly in your role to see which areas of yours are underperforming and need adjustment, using data (see above).

The key element in all of the above is a willingness *to learn*. If you want to be a startup leader, don't fret if you don't have all of the skills and experience at this very moment in time, because, in reality, no one does before doing the job. You can do it and learn along the way. (We'll talk about the "how" for addressing skill gaps in the next chapters.)

The phrase "growth mindset" coined by Carol Dweck is a Silicon Valley favorite for a reason; it's crucial for people at any role in a startup to learn, adapt, and grow, but the executive especially must grow their abilities as their startup grows.

Empactr co-founder and CEO Chris Senesi says the key skill he looks for in startup leaders is that they, above all, are initiators.

"I like when an individual is passionate about something and they champion it," said Senesi. "Taking initiative and ownership in an area builds trust. Leaders then get to create something new and show their skills and expertise. You don't have to be a startup founder to initiate."

This leads to the next big takeaway for "essential skills and experience" in startup leaders: prior "big-company" or other scaling startup expertise.

MANY SCALING STARTUPS BRING IN LEADERS FROM BIG COMPANIES

As they mature, it's common for startups to bring in leaders from big companies who've proven they've owned a function or profit and loss statement (P&L)

successfully before. Once startups get out of what investor and Harvard Business School professor Jeff Bussgang refers to as "the Jungle" stage of startup growth, they're often compelled by the board to bring in "adults" (the phrase makes me cringe, but it's common parlance) who can steer the ship as trained specialists.

In some ways, it's a catch-22; often you can't get the startup leadership job until you've proven you can do it, and you can't prove you can do it until you've done it. Where does that leave the contributors who've been mid-level managers at multiple startups, with valuable expertise, but not necessarily that full executive title?

We'll talk about how to make that transition if you don't bring that "experienced big-company person" background to your startup leadership journey. For now, let's focus on the startup executive who is a serial "big company" person from a larger organization. If you're coming from a larger company, you may have the expertise your startup needs but will have to learn to adapt to a high-growth environment.

EXECUTIVE COACH AND FORMER MICROSOFT NORTH AMERICA CFO JOHN REX: ADVICE FOR SCALING STARTUP LEADERS

Executive coach John Rex was a CFO at Microsoft prior to transitioning to a startup and now coaches leaders of all company sizes. He notes that it's a common challenge for scaling startups to help their "big company" leaders adapt and thrive.

"Many people are ideally suited, not to thrive and do a great job at a startup, but a big company," says Rex.

In large companies, you're incentivized to hone skills primarily around decision-making without much execution, often in markets that are already established.

"The skill that you really develop is how to decide what's important because there's so much information flowing toward you, so many requests for your time," says Rex. "You get really good at sifting through large volumes of incoming information. That isn't your remit at a startup that's disrupting a new market," says Rex.

Leaders coming from larger companies can underestimate the impact of having less structure and fewer resources, which was something Rex himself struggled with coming from Microsoft to a smaller startup.

"I really didn't appreciate the magnitude of how different those cultures are," says Rex. "For founders I coach, I now tell them, you want to be super careful when you hire big company executives because they just don't know what they don't know. They are used to being very successful but it's in a particular context of success. What is required for success in a startup environment is very different from what's required for success in a large corporation."

"At a big company, I spent most of my time in email and meetings because that's how I processed the vast amount of information that flowed toward me. At a startup, I had to return to practicing skills that I had come to delegate to more junior people in my corporate days," says Rex.

Leveling down isn't about lack of willingness or a "holier than thou" attitude. Rather, many big company leaders just haven't done it for a long time.

SCALING IS HARD IN BOTH DIRECTIONS

The reason why so many seasoned leaders are brought in as a startup matures is that scalability is hard in *both* directions. If you've never been a leader at a mature organization, it's a learning curve to get out of the day-to-day tactical operations. Many startup leaders struggle with this. (We'll discuss some very practical tips for addressing it.)

Early-stage startup people develop a skill set that is heavily tactical and geared towards "firefighting." This involves building functions from scratch and implementing basic processes as well as blocking and tackling, dealing with crises, unexpected challenges, and more.

LEARN TO DELEGATE WITH CAPABLE TALENT AS YOU SCALE

In addition to learning how to delegate, startup leaders need to accurately assess the talent and experience of their teams to understand whether the people they hire have what it takes to mature with the company. The more capable your team, the more you can delegate to them. If they are less capable, you will do more yourself. If you don't have people capable enough, then you're perpetually caught doing everything yourself. Many people burn out due to this (including founders who haven't brought in scalable leaders). You need a team you can truly rely on to do the work now and also help the company grow.

The more successful a leader becomes, the more they need to learn to get things done through others. Leaders can't continue to do everything themselves because that doesn't scale. You have to delegate work to your team.

Just as it's hard for an executive coming from a big company to scale down and do the tactical work, it is difficult for people from startup backgrounds to scale up because they're used to executing and being the ones to solve something. It doesn't come naturally to those of us used to the dopamine rush of being firefighters or those early doers, but it's essential to learn this skill to scale your team and your department's impact alongside you.

EARLY-STAGE STARTUP VS. SCALE-UP LEADERSHIP MINDSET

Executive coach and author Gerry Valentine says he often coaches startup leaders from big companies on shifting their mentality and mindset to become comfortable with disruption. Disruption is generally discouraged in those environments but is crucial at startups.

"In big corporations, you are paid specifically not to break things. If you're working for an American Express and you break something, the stock price might shift. You might make the cover of the *Wall Street Journal*. That's really bad," says Valentine.

Startup leaders aren't necessarily paid for moving fast and breaking things (a phrase coined in the early days of Facebook), but they are expected to experiment and iterate to drive success.

"In the early days, you're there to learn so your startup can grow faster," says Valentine. "The mistake I've seen leaders make coming from startups that are scaling up is that they fall in love with disruptive creativity. This matters in early stages, but not in the same way later on."

STARTUP LEADERS CAN'T GET STUCK AT 30,000 FEET

"We have all seen the leaders who are at 30,000 feet and they're not aware of what's really happening," says Gainsight CEO Nick Mehta. "I think some people misunderstand that being an executive means we know even *more* of the details."

At Apple, every leader is expected to know everything about Apple.[4] As a startup executive, you need to understand the details and not lose sight of them while also holding the bigger picture. Being both a tactical, hands-on builder when necessary and a strategic leader who can empower their team to deliver the next stage of growth is an unbeatable competitive advantage, and in the following chapters we're going to discover how you can make it yours.

CHAPTER TWO

Bridging the Transition from Manager to Executive: How Leaders Got Their First Role

> *If you want to be a startup executive, there are several skill and experience gaps you'll likely need to address to make the transition. Here's how some successful startup leaders did it.*

The skills and experience gaps you'll need to address to transition to an executive are within your reach. To be a strategic leader who can scale, you'll need to operate differently from how you did in prior roles. In this chapter, we'll discuss how leaders landed their first startup roles and how they successfully bridged the transition.

MAKING THE LEADERSHIP TRANSITION: YOU DON'T HAVE TO BE "FULLY READY" TO GO FOR IT

"I think we have this story that we need to wait to be knighted with a K to be in leadership," says VC and executive coach Sue Heilbronner. "Instead, just go identify an objective and start working towards it until you're doing it. Deciding to do leadership is that simple."

HOW THEY GOT THEIR FIRST EXECUTIVE ROLE: REAL STORIES FROM STARTUP EXECUTIVES

Rachel Beisel spent years as a marketing manager in the outdoor industry before pivoting to technology marketing, eventually becoming promoted from Director to VP at her company (she's since become a C-level executive at another technology company). She credits the help of a mentor in making the leap, including learning how to navigate the startup environment and become an executive.

Samantha McKenna is an accomplished sales leader, former VP of Sales at LinkedIn and On24, and now runs a consulting firm called Sam Sales. In her first executive role, she was promoted from within her organization. She said one of the challenges to making the leap from individual sales contributor to sales executive was, ironically, her high performance as a rep.

"In many organizations that lack forward-thinking growth, they do not want to lose the revenue that you, as an individual contributor, bring for the organization," says McKenna. "They want to keep you in your role, with the millions of dollars that you bring in every year."

McKenna says the key to getting promoted was to master doing her current job while also starting to take on the ownership and "stretching" beyond the role simultaneously.

"For anybody that wants to get promoted, ask yourself, how do I do the job that I was hired to do very well, and then how do I stretch myself beyond that? I needed to prove that I could proactively do more, not just by taking instruction, but by looking for gaps in the business and ways that I could contribute my skill set to fix those issues," says McKenna.

For McKenna, after two-and-a-half years of being highly successful, coming in first place numerous times for crushing her sales quota, she decided to go for the executive seat.

"I really had my sights set on leadership and I had a leader in October of a particular year who promised me that if I finish the year off successfully that I could get promoted. In November of that year, the executive was fired," says McKenna.

McKenna says that when she went to his replacement the following January, it took her three months to even get the conversation on the books. Despite having finished the previous year as the second highest performing member of the sales team, by April she had fallen behind in her quota and was told that she couldn't get promoted given her Q1 performance, and would need to prove herself. Again. The lesson she learned: regardless of the relationship you have with leadership, get commitments in writing. Further, this was a call to action to leadership. Promotions and honors shouldn't only be based on an individual having proven themselves; it should also be based on the potential one sees in someone.

"I had to hustle, but I had to carve out this role for myself. So I had to not only carve the role out for myself but then prove I was worth it twice," says McKenna.

MINDY LAUCK ON BEING A NON-FOUNDER STARTUP TEAM MEMBER PROMOTED TO EXECUTIVE, AND THEN CEO (TWICE!)

Mindy Lauck, CEO of Broadly, has been in two situations where she's not the founder but made her way up to CEO. She's been a non-founder CEO both times she's been CEO (at About.me and Broadly), and by being promoted to suddenly inheriting a board, executive team, and company.

"I inherited my executives, the team, everything was pre-made," says Lauck. "Founders don't have to deal with this," says Lauck.

Lauck assessed the startup phase they were in, understanding the state of the startup and whether certain executives and programs were right for their stage.

"I tried to really think about what phase are we in, what phase are we going to, and are these the right people for the right phase?" says Lauck.

Lauck had to adapt the mindset of executives who are non-founders and make the best of the situation she inherited while focusing on contributing her strengths to grow the business.

"You're not doing the business a favor if you wait too long to make those decisions, especially when it's at the executive level," says Lauck. "I let go of the executives that weren't the right fit, and focused on building trust and communication as well as aligning around values with the team that stayed."

Lauck credits her swift action with her success in the role, and being promoted again to CEO, since she had a proven track record.

CHALLENGE FOR FIRST-TIME EXECUTIVES: SAM MCKENNA SHARES HER STORY OF BEING PROMOTED TO VICE PRESIDENT OF SALES

On her path to her first executive role, entrepreneur and sales leader Sam McKenna was a director and then promoted to senior director before being promoted to Vice President. McKenna said she learned to advocate for herself while acknowledging that she was hired instead of a few team members who never quite accepted her in her new role.

McKenna overcame obstacles around this by focusing on empowering her team and proving she could build and manage a high-performing sales organization. Knowing she "had their back" created a lot of trust and the foundation for her team to consistently exceed their goals.

"I really made a point of building my brand around success not at the expense of others," says McKenna. "I let my team know, it's not a dog-eat-dog situation; it's we-win or we-die as a team."

McKenna also had to work on building new relationships cross-functionally thich she did not have to do as an individual contributor.

"As a top performer, I know I made a lot of demands of our legal team, including 'I want it and I want it now.' Patience is a word I still don't understand," says McKenna.

In her leadership role, she had to make new inroads with that team, taking time to invest in cross-functional leaders in a way she had not before.

McKenna says a common mistake she sees in scaling leaders who are trying to make the leap from director to VP is focusing on the wrong things to get promoted and/or letting their performance in their current roles slip.

"The sales reps that I speak to say, 'Well, I hit 75 percent of quota the last three years, but I also created a birthday club last year . . . shouldn't that get me promoted,'" says McKenna. "I tell them, what matters first is the consistency at which you exceed your goals. You have to nail the job you were hired to do first, before you highlight anything else you've done above-and-beyond. Once that's underway, what you do to stretch yourself has to address the goals your executives are focused on; take the time to understand what your executives are trying to solve and then help them get there," says McKenna.

If you don't do what you're paid to do exceptionally well, it's hard to make the case that you'll be more successful once promoted.

"Be the top of your class and then stretch yourself. And when you stretch yourself, it needs to be solving issues that are economic issues that are top-tier issues for your executives," says McKenna.

Before getting promoted to her first executive role, McKenna took time to interview her EVP of Sales. She committed to helping him solve his problems, and asked him, "what does success look like for you this year?"

When he told her attrition and not ramping fast enough, Sam took it upon herself to solve it as an executive would, even though she wasn't one yet.

She focused on making people on her team feel like "more than a number" so they wouldn't leave and creating an onboarding and mentorship program so that they ramped faster. Then she tracked it so she could prove the ROI.

"No one's sitting around telling you what's keeping them up at night, so you have to find out," says McKenna. "Taking extreme ownership of the 'stay up at night' problems is the key to going from a director or manager to a true executive."

MAKING THE TRANSITION BY LEARNING TO WORK DIFFERENTLY

The level of execution you'll do as a startup leader depends on the size and scale of your organization. You may be years away from being able to delegate. In the early stages of building a sales function, for example, as the executive, you may be standing up some of the processes and/or using tools like a sales enablement platform and CRM in a hands-on way. But once you scale, you'll hire a sales ops manager, and/or outsource this to another member of your team. Becoming clear what tasks would change around you moving to director or executive is important.

FROM BIG COMPANY LEADER TO STARTUP EXECUTIVE: COO ERIN RAND'S STORY

For operations executive Erin Rand, COO of PlasticBank, her first executive role was at a larger organization and her first startup executive role came later. At the larger organization, a rapidly-scaling company of thousands of employees, she described her first-time executive experience as "getting my ticket punched."

"The first time you're in an executive role is the hardest to make happen because it's the first person who's willing to take that chance on you," says Rand. "Once you've had the title, everybody else sees you as that from then on."

Rand was given her first executive role, which involved owning a business line with profit and loss (P&L), because she had proven herself successful as a manager and the mentors around her helped her succeed and believed in her ability to learn and grow into an executive role.

"One of the key things of being successful is having a close group of people around you who support your growth," says Rand. "I had a group of people around me who were very generous with their support and their advice."

Rand once had a global controller let her know she'd behaved in a meeting in a way that didn't land well. She would start meetings jumping right into the work without making small talk, which he said didn't align with the organization's mode of operating and culture.

"He told me to take time to connect with everybody who's in the room and have a human conversation," says Rand. "I thought that we're all under this time pressure and how I'm being judged is what I get done, and people are expecting me to deliver results. I don't want to waste people's time."

Rand's mentor helped her realize that leadership wasn't just about delivering results, but about establishing the relationships in the organization, building trust, not just in your own team, but your peers and others. Everybody wants to be seen.

By taking in feedback from mentors around her and applying it, she ended up being promoted to take over an organization of more than 80 people with tens of millions in revenue.

"The CEO didn't believe that I should be given the role because it was such a big jump for me," says Rand. "I'd only ever led a single-digit team, but my mentor convinced him I would perform."

Rand's first executive role at a large company led her to become a startup executive, and she faced some of the growing pains discussed earlier of mapping her "big company" experience to a highly different startup culture. She says her friends and even some of her supporters at her larger company doubted her ability to successfully transition.

"You're like Ms. Corporate," they told me. "Oh, you're going to hate it. You're not going to be good at it," says Rand.

Rand ignored the naysayers and found a group of peers in Silicon Valley focused on women's empowerment in business who encouraged her to talk about her contributions rather than her role. When she met a startup founder who had an open operations leadership role, she was able to successfully describe how her experience at a big company would support his scaling startup.

"Instead of saying I was a senior director of global services, I would say, 'I figure out how to build organizations that don't exist or break down and rebuild organizations that need to be rebuilt in a fast-moving way.'"

Upon transitioning from big-company executive to startup executive, Rand says it took time to "knock the corporate off (her)." Rand learned to integrate more of her personal life with her professional persona at a startup, becoming more vulnerable with her team, and even befriending them on social media. While acclimatization to startup culture required effort, she also found that her skills and "big company" knowledge were highly valuable in the startup environment and she found success by leaning on those early on.

She quickly found a home for her honed operations skills based on the startup's needs. Rand was very comfortable with board meetings and prep due to lots of early exposure at her large company.

"In my first leadership role at a startup, I saw what they were sharing with the board. I was like, 'what the F--- are you doing? This is a mess. How can this be what you're sharing with the board?"

Rand spent the week prior to her first board meeting re-doing all of the company's materials, including the financials and reporting structure. The board was "very happy" with the results of her efforts, and that the founder had someone who could communicate in the way the board expected and who could structure the information in a way they could understand and give feedback on much more efficiently.

Rand says she had a "really firm wall" between her personal and professional lives. In her larger company environment, she learned it was "unprofessional" to blend the two. When she started getting social media invitations from her global team members at the startup, she was nervous. One of her direct reports told her they wanted to know her and for her to know them, and she took that feedback to heart.

"Now, I understand there's never anything more important than the people around you, so it doesn't matter what deadline you're on. If someone comes up to your desk and wants to talk, you just stop and you talk. You don't make them feel like you're rushed," says Rand.

NAIL THE LEAP: START AS A "HEAD OF" AND MAKE THE TITLE OFFICIAL ONCE YOU'VE PROVEN YOUR SUCCESS

In Matt Mochary's book *The Great CEO Within*, contributor Alex MacCaw advocates that CEOs bring on "heads of" to start in their new ventures. "Call everyone 'head of x.' That way, when it's finally time to hire senior VPs, they can slot easily into the organization without 'demoting' anyone."[1]

Here's where the biggest opportunity lies for first-time startup executives, particularly those looking to level up within their current organizations. Go for the head of role, use the guides in this book (and lots of elbow grease) to earn your first executive seat.

CONSULTING AS A PATH TO DE-RISKING YOUR FIRST EXECUTIVE ROLE

On my path to becoming a startup executive, I inadvertently stumbled upon a career accelerant: consulting. Underrepresented minorities who aren't seen with perceived potential due to systemic bias and don't yet have past performance track records need to find a way to bridge that gap. Consulting can be that bridge.

I'd been a multi-time director at several startups when I was in between companies after an exit and decided to do some consulting while looking for my next opportunity. I applied for director level as well as head of marketing jobs on a whim. In some companies, "head of" is the stand-in that can mean everything from senior manager up to CMO, so I wasn't necessarily applying for executive roles.

This was also around the time when I had that fateful VC conversation mentioned in the introduction. After that, I started billing myself as a "fractional marketing leader for hire," which many early-stage startups interpreted as startup marketing executive. Without anyone's permission, I started doing executive-level marketing work for startups, building their go-to-market strategies from the ground up. There were things I didn't know how to do and I got paid as a consultant to learn how to do them for my clients without any of the pressure of "being an executive." I just did the role!

My consulting journey involved learning how to create marketing budgets and annual planning spreadsheets (thank you, former boss and spreadsheet guru Matt Harada, for coaching me through this!). I learned how to build and scale-up marketing functions quickly for my clients in order to earn their repeat business. One of my consulting clients was acquired by a public company after we worked together for about four months, and then I began working with three new clients, all three of whom eventually offered me full-time roles at the "head of marketing" or "VP of marketing" title. Just like that, my clients saw me as a head of the department, and I joined one of them. Six months later I asked for and got a promotion to vice president after proving I was already succeeding in that role.

"If you can afford to consult, you can do a three-month trial to see if you really love the job before you take it. I appreciate the approach of trying an opportunity first as you find your executive fit," says customer success executive Emilia D'Anzica.

If you're a director and/or a "head of" and want to be a true executive, consulting can be a great way to "live the reality you want" and to de-risk it to give yourself a chance to be successful without the pressure of jumping into it full-time.

The worst that can happen is you decide to go back to being a mid-level manager if and when you join somewhere full-time. Not everyone can comfortably do consulting without guaranteed business or health insurance, etc., so you'll have to assess your situation and whether you can transition into leadership through this modality. In my case, I'd already had a consulting practice and an LLC I could use between full-time jobs, including the legal paperwork from when I'd consulted with different levels of experience.

Jennifer Rice, who creates learning programs at Pavilion, a member organization for supporting revenue leaders, builds courses to help professionals transition into their first executive-level roles and succeed once they're there. Rice sees firsthand how "associates" grow into executive roles through getting hands-on training and access to a supportive community of peers and mentors.

Many aspiring executives don't get exposed to executive responsibilities in their current jobs, meaning they don't often come across a stretch project that goes into executive territory. This is unlike stretch assignments in other areas of your department or other functions. Pavilion teaches aspiring leaders storytelling with data, financial modeling, and other skills that are required for startup executives, giving them an opportunity to gain a foothold.

Whether it's through consulting, taking a course at an organization like Pavilion, or learning while in your current role, you can find the skills you need to become successful and will only truly know how it is for you once you give it a shot. Here's your friendly sign from the universe that you deserve to take that shot.

CHAPTER THREE

Understanding and Evaluating Your Fit at Various Startups

> *A common cause of startup executive failure: taking a role that's a bad fit. Here's how to avoid that and find the right fit for you.*

CHOOSING A STARTUP THAT'S RIGHT FOR YOU

Startups vary based on stage, size, maturity, location, founding team, company values, and market. If you're a startup leader at a scaling venture, many of these attributes will change over the course of your startup as it grows. When evaluating a new opportunity, decide what's most important to you and ask questions to confirm that the opportunity aligns with what you're looking for, knowing that you may need to re-evaluate during key moments in your startup's life.

WHY QUESTIONS MATTER

As you ask questions exploring startup fit, the answers say a lot about the type of company you're being interviewing at, and whether or not it will appeal to you. Expect that there will be some underwhelming or even disappointing answers to some of the questions you ask. Remember, every startup has issues. That's why they are hiring you: to help make it better. The point of asking lots of questions is to know the priority issues of the business that you can solve, as well as whether the values and priorities of the business are aligned with your own. Don't be shy about asking financial questions. If you're taking a pay cut for a role, it's fair to want to understand what the equity is worth and what the company's long-term priorities are.

For example, is the company planning to take a big bet and raise hundreds of millions of dollars and either be the next unicorn chasing a massive total addressable market (TAM) or become a huge crater in the ground? Maybe they are more measured and are going to grow at a slower clip while building the product or they have methodically owned a particular corner of a smaller market. Once you've identified which environment you want to be in, you can listen to the answers to help you assess the fit.

SOME SAMPLE QUESTIONS TO EXPLORE IN THE INTERVIEW PROCESS

- What is the company's fundraising status?
- What is the target market and total addressable market (TAM) and serviceable addressable market (SAM)?
- What's the annual sales price (ASP)?
- Is there a product–market fit or is there a path to it?
- What's the cost per acquisition (CAC) right now (ballparks are okay)?
- What's the Net Promoter Score (NPS) and Net Revenue Retention (NRR)?
- What are the company's long-term goals (or longer-termish)?
- Who's the ideal customer profile (ICP)?
- Who else is on the leadership team? What's the plan for scaling the organization?
- What's the capitalization table like? What's the company's exit plan (if they have one)?
- When does the company plan to raise again?
- What's the company's cash position?

OTHER CONSIDERATIONS

What's the Market and What's the Problem the Company Is Solving (and Do You Care?)

These are ed tech, manufacturing, entertainment, construction, cloud hosting, Content Delivery Network (CDN), and on. So many markets within tech startups! What do you want to do? Who do you want to sell to? What impact do you want to make? Do you want to sell to the enterprise or SMB or schools or government? You need to think about it. Selling B2B? B2C? B2B2C? B2G?

RESEARCH THE COMPETITION/MARKET

As a startup leader, you'll need to have an opinion about the market, regardless of whether you're in product, customer success, marketing, sales, finance, or another department. As your startup matures, it may pivot, but understanding the "space" you're in helps you tell the story about the contributions you'll make on behalf of the business.

RESEARCH THE TEAM THROUGH YOUR CONNECTIONS AND/OR PUBLIC REVIEW SITES LIKE LINKEDIN AND GLASSDOOR

They're going to be doing research on you; find out who your colleagues will be, where they've worked before, and look at the company's reputation on social sites. While not all information will be up-to-date, you can glean a surprising amount from a little digital sleuthing. Find commonalities, mutual connections, and anything that can help you understand the people with whom you'd be working.

ASSESS THE CO-FOUNDER RELATIONSHIP

According to relationship expert, therapist, and author Esther Perel, at least 65% of startups fail due to the relationship between co-founders.[1] Perel's research highlights that positive co-founder relationships are crucial for successful companies. Try to find out about the co-founder relationship prior to joining; see how long they've worked together, whether they've worked together before, and are they respectful of one another's areas of expertise.

"Starting a company is like being in a marriage," says entrepreneur, engineering, and operations leader Evan Hung.

"Co-founding a company requires all of the work of what it looks like to be in a marriage and that means understanding values and standing where you want to go with things, and knowing how to navigate conflict because conflict is actually inevitable. It's not a matter of if you fight. It's a matter of when and how frequently and how aggressively. Join a founding team that you believe will do this well and can get the company to the next stage of growth," says Hung.

An increasingly common co-founder combination is one technical co-founder who owns Product, Engineering, and sometimes support, and one business co-founder who owns the go-to-market including sales, customer success, and marketing. Each owns their respective business areas with relative autonomy, but this isn't always the case.

Of the five startups I've worked for that have successfully exited, four of them had co-founders (one was a solo founder), and they had notably strong co-founder relationships. Delegation of responsibilities was clear, their relationships were prioritized, and, for what it's worth, they all seemed to genuinely like and care about each other as people. Look for indicators that co-founders have worked successfully together before, know each other very well, and accept each other's strengths and flaws. If you ask questions upfront, you can hopefully avoid finding yourself in the middle of a messy founder drama.

UNDERSTAND THE STARTUP'S STAGE AND HOW IT ALIGNS WITH YOUR GOALS

Jeffrey Bussgang is an entrepreneur, investor, Harvard Business School Professor, and author of the book *Entering Startupland*.

He describes three stages of startup life:

- "Jungle"—pre-product/market fit (around 1–50 employees).
- "Dirt Road"—post-product/market fit, pre-scaling sales and marketing (around 50–250 employees).
- "Highway"—post-scaling sales and marketing (around 250–5k employees).[2]

Bussgang describes the "Jungle" stage as being pre-product-market fit, where the business is full of unknowns and generally "high risk" when it comes to success guarantees. *Do we even have a scalable, viable business model?* is a question that startups often need to ask themselves in this phase.

The "Dirt Road" defines the stage at which the startup journey is somewhat clear, but it's windy and bumpy. This stage is post-product-market fit, yet still early in repeatable sales and marketing. The founder may still be heavily involved in sales, annual recurring revenue isn't as predictable as established companies, but there's some proven market traction and usually banner customers on board at this stage.

In the "Highway" stage, companies are post-sales and marketing post-product-market fit. Think of this as the "scaling" stage where companies frequently grace the headlines as hyper-growth technology companies, not *can-they-do-it* startups out to prove themselves. The proof at that point is in the pudding (or, to be more specific, market capitalization).

"Once you're on the highway, it's very smooth and repeatable," says Bussgang. "You're flying along trying to get all the systems running, achieve profitability, and make those unit economics really sing."

Bussgang says that different people are wired differently in terms of what excites them and how much risk they're willing to take.

"Those are the two dimensions that I would encourage people to think about," says Bussgang. "First, decide what excites you, whether that's pre-product market fit and being more product- or technically-oriented, or if you'd love figuring out the stage of repeatable sales and marketing, or if you love figuring out a profitable, highly scalable model. Second, think about risk: are you willing to take a lot of risk, a medium amount of risk, or more modest risk? That decision depends on your risk appetite and where you are in your life," says Bussgang.

DO YOU ALIGN WITH THE LEADERSHIP TEAM?

You need to align with your colleagues enough to want to put in a lot of time together tackling challenges. It can be difficult to get to know people before working with them, but it's worth doing due diligence and seeing the cohort you'd be joining and partnering with if you become serious about an opportunity. Some ideas: go on their professional social media like Twitter and LinkedIn and see how they communicate, chat with mutual connections, and gather data as you would on any other aspect of the company. You will get a better sense of what it will be like to collaborate.

OTHER KINDS OF FIT TO LOOK OUT FOR

Things like net promoter score (NPS score), product-market fit, sales and user growth, and funding status are measures of the growth of a business. Understanding your alignment with these indicators matters, but just as important, I believe, are the qualitative ones that have to do with fit. You'll never succeed at a company if it's not a great fit, but a great fit can help you make the most positive and successful impact possible.

SOME EXAMPLES OF FIT

- Company values that are aligned with your personal values.
- A company where you feel connected to the product and customer base; maybe you can personally relate to the challenges the startup solves or the consumer base or have extensive experience working in the space.
- A strong potential relationship with the team/co-founders.

- Can you bring your whole self to work (i.e. is their representation of different kinds of people, is the startup oriented towards individuality and inclusivity, and/or does everyone seem like a "mini me" of the founding team)?

I once worked for a company where I thought highly of the CEO and conceptually was very on board with the company's mission, but I didn't feel a strong connection to our target market or their problems. I couldn't relate to them, even though I tried to develop empathy for their challenges. It was my least favorite startup job, even though I was paid a great salary and, on paper, the role was a good fit for my skills and background. I performed well, and it boosted my career, but I was much happier once I left and started working on problems and solving for a target market I cared about more.

ASSESS THE MATURITY OF YOUR STARTUP'S DIVERSITY AND INCLUSION

Leaders who come from underrepresented backgrounds need to understand that there will be challenges anywhere we go, because oppression and "isms" exist in society and no startup exists in a bubble.

A self-described queer Latina disabled startup executive, Aubrey Blanche, shares the following advice for leaders who are evaluating the inclusiveness of an organization's culture:

"Everybody has their own tolerance for microaggressions and the oppressions that they face in any given job," says Blanche. "It would be a lie to tell underrepresented leaders that you're not going to run into that at work. So the question becomes: 'to what degree am I willing to put up with the bullsh-t? What level of organizational dysfunction am I able to accept?'"

Blanche says that minority leaders face an additional "tax" by needing to consider the impact of multiple forms of oppression every day at work, whereas leaders from dominant groups don't necessarily need to in the same way.

"There can be alienation as a leader from a "minoritized" background, because most of the people already in those rooms either don't share a value set of experiences with 'minoritized' leaders," says Blanche.

WHAT'S YOUR STARTUP-STAGE RISK TOLERANCE?

If you're joining a seed-stage of series A company, the upside (potential reward) is higher for your equity, but you'll come in likely at a lower base (also known as a "salary haircut"), and there's no guarantee your equity will be worth something, or that your liquidity event will happen any time soon. Whereas at a publicly-traded company RSUs have a clear value and liquidity, so early-stage equity is much riskier. According to Carta, women employees own $0.49 in equity to every dollar a man owns.[3]

Most early-stage companies are less likely to agree to an executive salary at the level of series B and beyond, so if you're truly wanting a higher cash compensation to reduce your risk, it's tough to find top-dollar startup roles prior to Series B.

You can mitigate your risk coming in early by asking for a contractual agreement around "true-upping" your cash to market rates at key revenue or fundraising milestones.

HOW MUCH EXECUTION AND "GETTING YOUR HANDS DIRTY" ARE YOU COMFORTABLE WITH RIGHT AWAY?

How much execution will you do based on company maturity? In a Series A company, a head of marketing will spend a lot of time in the weeds, doing things like scheduling blog posts, revising white papers, setting up marketing automation campaigns, calling vendors to confirm pricing, and taking out the proverbial trash. This changes upon scale; you will be more focused on empowering others to do the work. If you try to be a VP of Sales at a seed or series A startup having not dusted off Salesforce in years other than a dashboard view someone in ops built for you, that's going to take some adjustment. While you can't get too far away from tactical understanding (if not execution) completely in later stages, know that you'll be expected to do a lot of heavy lifting yourself when you join an early-stage company.

If you are a head of sales and you've been successful as an individual account executive and always crushed quota but never scaled a team of reps or run a play-book to scale to $20 million in ARR, that's going to be tough. Any leaps with two or more steps outside your zone will require you to think differently about success and achievement. Finding the right stage of startup maturity where you can take what you're already good at and use it to grow will set you and your startup heading for success.

A first-time head of sales who's hit several million dollars per year quota for the target market and average sales price (ASP) the company is selling may be a great fit to be the first non-founder sales leader at a company that's on its path to the first million in ARR, and can learn how to build process around it to scale a team on the way. Not easy, but is more doable than coming in with that back-ground and trying to help a company go from $1 million ARR to $15 million ARR having never done it before or scaled a team.

For example, for my first startup executive role, I joined as "head of" for a target market and ASP I'd worked in for more than a decade. I was a subject matter expert in everything but the role, and I learned the part of the role I needed to as I went. This would have been harder had I tried to join a later-stage startup, or one outside my market experience.

Try to make the leaps manageable and within your comfort zone to set your-self up for maximum success.

DETERMINING YOUR IDEAL STARTUP STAGE

Earlier-stage startups are a good way to break into leadership if you've never done it before because they're as pre-scale as you are. If you can prove you can scale, that's a great way to "get in" on the early stage, get equity, and grow with the com-pany through its maturity.

Jeff Bussgang, VC and author, says being a part of a start-up or a growth stage company as a joiner, most typically it's your first time as an executive, and so you need to develop three things simultaneously:

1. An understanding of the company's domain and market dynamics
2. Expertise in your functional area (Customer Success, Sales, Marketing, Operations, etc.), including the modern best practices that are cutting-edge in the industry
3. Executive and leadership skills (including topics discussed in this book)

Bussgang says that all three are hard to find in an individual leader. You can absolutely pursue a role at a growth stage company, but at that later stage, boards often want the founders to look for someone who has "done it before" and can demonstrate they've mastered each of these areas. When hiring a Chief Revenue Officer (CRO) or VP of sales, a Series B startup will look for that person who's proven they've built a team, coached them successfully, and got the company to repeatable, substantial sales revenue.

"When a customer is unhappy, certain things happen and then they reliably churn," says Bussgang. "You want to look at the leading indicators, which are more like usage or net promoter score or number of logins and time on task and time in the app. Those are all leading indicators of customer happiness with a product as opposed to the lagging indicator of churn."

"I don't care if your revenue is zero and stays zero for two years if you're learning a lot and can show how what you're learning is contributing to building equity value," says Bussgang.

CHAPTER FOUR

Landing Your Next Startup Executive Role: Leveling Up Within Your Current Organization or Seeking a Role Elsewhere

> *Can you become an executive within your current startup? That depends--*
> *here are the scenarios where it's possible, and a couple where you probably*
> *won't get there, at least not anytime soon. Plus, how to look for your next*
> *startup executive role outside your current organization.*

Are you looking to level up to your first leadership role from within your current startup? This chapter features in-the-trenches stories of managers or directors or "head of" startup contributors who made the transition to executive, what they did to prepare themselves, how they made the case, plus a true story of how I successfully landed my first executive promotion after a shockingly brief (ten-minute!) discussion that was seven months in the making!

Many first-time startup executives join as "head of" and prove they're able to be a true executive. This path aligns with the industry's common advice for founders from VCs and accelerators on how to level their early-stage leadership team.

MY FIRST EXECUTIVE ROLE: JOINING AN EARLY-STAGE STARTUP AND GETTING PROMOTED TO VP

My first executive role involved a "head of" where I proved I could own all of marketing and then was promoted to the executive title after six months. Prior to this, I'd done consulting in "head of" capacities where I tried out different functional marketing areas ranging from the strategic to the tactical.

That conversation to go from "head of" to "VP" took all of ten minutes. I asked my CEO to make me VP and shared the metrics highlighting my performance from the past six months. I asked him not to hire someone above me in marketing, but to make my title vice president. My CEO told me I should have asked for the title sooner, because he already saw me as an executive! It turned out, being a 'head of' and doing the role, which was preceded by consulting, was a great path for me.

To do this, it's crucial to set your intentions and let your CEO (or direct manager) know what you're aiming for. Let them know you don't want to be hired over and discover their expectations for you and for the role. If they're clear that they want to bring in a seasoned VP or CFO at series A or B, for example, you should know that. If they're open to you ascending into the role, you'll have a clearer path on how to get there.

HOW ANALIESE BROWN, VP OF PEOPLE AT CAMPMINDER, GOT PROMOTED INTO HER FIRST EXECUTIVE STARTUP ROLE

Analiese Brown, VP of People at CampMinder, landed her first executive role as the head of HR at a self-funded startup called ShipCompliant. She didn't initially join the company as a member of the executive team—she entered via mid-management and earned her leadership seat from within. When she initially came aboard, the company was on its way to $10 million in ARR, but was still forming its leadership team. At ShipCompliant, the highest title Brown ever held was "Director." However, as the highest-level HR professional, she transitioned into serving as a member of the executive team, even with a Director title.

"I certainly had influence and some level of authority, but I didn't have a seat at the executive table when I joined," said Brown.

Brown was the most senior HR professional in her organization as her responsibilities scaled alongside the company. She was eventually able to transition to an executive-level position by acting "as if" her role was already at the executive level. She didn't give up execution-focused duties, but she also took on higher-level strategic thinking for the business, incorporating this perspective into the function that she, de facto, began owning like an executive. She did this through aligning her promotion with the business' maturity in recognizing her function HR as a business imperative worthy of executive-level leadership.

Brown says that the existing executive team eventually realized as the business matured that "employee engagement," human resources, and People Ops needed a seat at the executive table. She'd helped the team understand that it would benefit every element of the business' bottom line to provide her organization with the HR and People Ops leadership it deserved.

How Brown scaled up to an executive role within her current company:

- **Tying her results to executive-level performance.** She helped the company identify that the organization she ran deserved a seat at the executive table by creating strategic initiatives that could be tied to business outcomes.
- **Proactive in taking ownership.** She took it upon herself to own the function and lead it, like an executive, before either she or her company officially recognized the need for and title of her de-facto role.
- **Communicated her results to the executive team.** She learned to "speak their language" so they saw her as one of their own, even before the promotion.
- **Took a "global view" in aligning her role to the business needs.** Brown developed strategic business positions around what they were trying to accomplish as a business and found ways that she could add value.
- **Learned more about areas of her function she had less experience in.** Brown gained an understanding of the areas of her function (People Ops) that she needed to be successful (HR, recruiting, headcount costs, benefits, and more).

"I had the opportunity for the couple of years that I was in that position before moving into an executive seat to really show that I could deliver not only on the areas that were already within my realm of accountability, but zooming out and identifying company objectives," says Brown.

Eventually, Brown's company was acquired. She credits being part of a smaller company where she wore many hats for being tapped for higher-level responsibilities than her formal job description.

Brown suggests rising leaders should ask the following questions when making the transition to executive-level leadership:

- What is the company trying to accomplish strategically?
- What is the company's vision at the highest level?
- What are the company's strategies and goals at the highest level and how can I add value and be responsive to those in my role and then be explicit about the ways that I was doing that?

- Can I be promoted if I accomplish the executive leadership goals that are important to the company?

To move from a Director to VP-level role at her current company, Brown researched job requirements descriptions for the functions at other similar-size companies, mapping what each role needed, making it clear that the roles were VP-level and in some cases C-level.

"I pitched that internally to my CEO and to the rest of the team and shared the research," says Brown.

Brown researched the differences between director, VP, and C-level responsibilities. She found sample job descriptions for each level of the people organization, and mapped that to the work that people were doing and what was said they were accountable for. She made the case for moving from a Director to VP role in her role at CampMinder.

"Knowing what my role needed to accomplish helped me make the case for it and when I presented it to my CEO," says Brown "it then was clearly kind of a no-brainer, an obvious shift for me to take the VP title since it wasn't that my responsibilities changed much."

Brown said once the company's organization chart "caught up" with the work she was doing, it was easy for her to have the team recognize her in that VP level and give her the title.

Though Brown had already been acting as a VP in many ways, the transition motivated her to level up further in several tactical and strategic areas:

- **Employee experience as a competitive advantage.** Brown looked not only at internal engagement but how her company performed against the market. "I asked myself, how can we create the best possible employee experience and also understand the talent market and external conditions that might be influencing the market? Let's make sure we look beyond our organization to understand the cultural and societal factors influencing the way people experience work and how they relate to work," says Brown.
- **Strategic understanding of her business including how her work would support the organization's position in the market.** She focused on where her organization and company wanted to position themselves relative to the market and then used that to make strategic decisions around how her work would serve the greater business goals. "It included the way we

shape our existing employees' experience to differentiate ourselves from competitors," says Brown.

- **Reporting to the board and other shareholders.** In both her roles at ShipCompliant and CampMinder, she learned how to speak to investors and explain the KPIs of her program in terms they understood, relating them to business goals.
- **Financial literacy applied to her People Ops department's strategy.** She learned to interpret and create basic budgets, especially a departmental budget, but in an executive-level seat, "I'm expected to digest and make sense of the company-wide budget and forecast and so really taking time to study to make sure I understood it and reach out to our CFO," says Brown.

GENERALIST TO SPECIALIST: HOW TO "COME UP" AS AN EXECUTIVE IN YOUR AREA OF SPECIALIZATION

I recently sat through a VP of sales candidate presentation in which the person delivered a pitch deck to our executive team. It was thorough, thoughtfully put together, and showed he'd listened to our business needs. If it were a real sales pitch, we would have been likely to buy. This is the power of a great sales leader who's also been a high-performing account executive (AE).

This leader in particular, however, needed to also show he could build and manage a team of AEs (and sales ops, and other areas) and was more than just an individual performer. He failed to do the latter, and we didn't end up hiring him. He was a great individual contributor (IC), but didn't prove to us he could scale into that stretch VP role. That candidate example shows that if you're a functional leader who can demonstrate proficiency in doing *and* in leading at a startup, you'll have job security.

LEARN TO BALANCE THE TACTICAL AND THE STRATEGIC

You need to understand markets and business areas that impact your startup, not only your particular role. Get "in the weeds" on a tactical level, understand the systems, tools, and key areas your organization covers, while also empowering others to execute so you don't do it all yourself.

Many aspiring startup leaders get stuck in the tactical zone and a surprising amount of current startup leaders struggle with the strategy if they can't understand how tactics rolls up to it.

Get comfortable with the high-level strategy and tactical details (even if you're not executing them yourself). This will make you a must-hire or must-promote if you can learn to provide value both at the high-level strategic and ground-floor tactical levels.

UNDERSTAND BUSINESS AREAS OUTSIDE YOUR "COMFORT ZONE"

A functional leader has to understand more programs than the narrow sliver that a mid-level manager might have. For example, if you're a director of demand generation, spend time understanding product marketing and/or content. If you're an individual contributor AE who wants to become a VP of sales, the next level could be a director of Sales or a sales manager, which can prepare you for becoming a VP and eventually even CRO.

If you're interested in growing into an executive role, think about how you can learn other areas of your function that you may not have owned previously. One way is to take on "stretch projects" outside of your area. Sometimes that's not possible in companies where these roles are already being fulfilled. To get around this, you can take a course online or consult in that area (get paid to learn).

EMBRACE A LEARNING OR "GROWTH" MINDSET

As Carol Dweck describes in her seminal book *Mindset,* learning is essential to growth. Read as much as you can in industry publications, listen to podcasts, attend webinars, and go to local and non-local meetups. (One virtue of the post-pandemic world is that we'll see more hybrid events.) There are groups that offer free educational meetups and many companies host user groups in localized areas (or online in virtual/hybrid formats).

"The game is not to get it right the first time," says leadership expert Anne Morriss. "The game is to learn as quickly as you can, and then react to that new insight. That learning muscle is not reliable nor intuitive for most of us walking the planet. Most of us have to pause and be deliberate about our growth."

If you're hoping to gain a skill or become more knowledgeable, teacher(s) can now be found in a variety of formats. It can help to find a buddy with whom to learn together, ideally a peer who's also hoping to gain skills in an area or grow their career. Be each other's peer supporters and help each other achieve your goals; you'll be surprised at how much more fun it is to bring someone else along with you as you both grow in your leadership roles.

HOW NICOLE WOJNO SMITH, VP OF MARKETING AT TACKLE, GOT HER FIRST EXECUTIVE ROLE BY LEVELING UP WITHIN HER THEN-ORGANIZATION

Nicole Wojno Smith, VP of Marketing at Tackle, leveled up to the CMO at a startup customer success SaaS company in Atlanta.

"They had a CRO in place that oversaw sales and marketing and after a few months of me being there, I was the senior director of marketing and they realized that maybe he wasn't really a CMO," says Smith. "And so I was already doing that work and I got promoted to CMO—skipping the VP title. I wasn't necessarily one to ask questions. I was just going to grab onto the reins and say, yes, I'm going to take this opportunity and run with it."

HOW SMITH "LEVELED UP" BY BUILDING A PARTNERSHIP WITH THE C-LEVEL TEAM

Smith credits her strong partnership with the CEO with her success in her first executive role.

"I realized that I was the steward of this brand. And our CEO and I discussed, how can we build this company together and take his vision for the company?"

Smith knew it was her responsibility to execute and align with her CEO on shared ideas and learn how to work successfully with her cross-functional executive peers.

"It was so important to work with all the other functions and let them provide buy-in on that plan and determine how we were going to work together to achieve those results," says Smith.

MASTERING DATA-DRIVEN STORYTELLING AROUND BUSINESS OBJECTIVES

Smith had a strong background in data and marketing funnel analytics, but in her first marketing executive role, she had to learn how to communicate this at the board level and make strategic decisions based on the numbers.

Smith says storytelling with analytics, whether in board meetings or to other executives, requires telling the story behind just the number. She interprets results and shows her program's return on investments and how they impact the strategic direction of the business.

GAIN A DEEPER UNDERSTANDING OF CROSS-FUNCTIONAL PART-NERS AND THEIR ROLES

Before becoming an executive marketing leader, Smith had prior sales knowledge. (Full disclosure: this included being married to a software sales leader.) She knew that to be a successful marketing leader, she needed to immerse herself in the sales world, including learning how to forecast and understand how marketing funnel indicators lead to sales results (revenue). Smith said she also invested in learning how to understand the product team's world.

"You have to really get in the trenches and you have to learn the product in order to market it effectively," says Smith.

PARTNER CLOSELY WITH YOUR FINANCE LEADERSHIP (UNLESS YOU'RE THE CFO; IN THAT CASE, PARTNER WITH EVERY OTHER EXECUTIVE TEAM)

Partnering with Finance and your CFO is crucial if you're a leader in a different department, because Finance sees into every aspect of the business operations. As you get higher up (and as companies get bigger), decisions become less about optimizing tactical execution and more about investing efforts in the right projects. Your finance leader can help you get that perspective.

No matter your department, rapport with the Finance team comes in handy. As you're demonstrating your results and plans at the highest altitude, you need to align your reporting with the metrics that the finance and board care most about. It's useful to have a partner to bounce your slides off before presenting them to ensure accuracy and alignment.

START UNOFFICIALLY RECRUITING YOUR "BENCH" DREAM TEAM FOR YOUR DEPARTMENT

Many leaders underestimate the challenge of convincing a stellar team to join you and follow you to your next company. You'll be many steps ahead if you can build a roster of people who would be great to collaborate with—peers or even folks who are a skip level below you on your previous teams, or perhaps partners whom you've encountered in the field.

If you are asked in an interview how you'll find and recruit talent, it helps to have a "warm" bench when you're on board. For instance, if you're in Sales and are a Sales Director looking to level up to VP, contact former account executives with whom you worked who may be willing to join you, as well as sales development reps (SDRS) you formerly managed, or Sales Ops and Enablement folks from your network.

Being helpful to your peer network, no matter your title, and creating the kind of relationships that people want to have at work based on trust, mutual respect, and action towards progress can set you up in a great place once you land.

First-time leaders explicitly or tacitly face the question "how can I trust you'll successfully hire a great team to scale your program if you've never done it?" Proactively building your talent bench helps you overcome the bias that often keeps people from getting their first executive role sooner.

LEVELING UP IN THE ENGINEERING SIDE OF THE BUSINESS: JEFF AMMONS

Jeff Ammons, who has been an early engineering leader at Slack and One Medical, entered a "world of chaos" early in his career in his first startup executive job. He was brought in to create scalable engineering processes as an individual contributor, and eventually got promoted to CTO.

"There was no onboarding documentation, we didn't have unit testing or a lot of good software industry best practices implemented," says Ammons. "We were just making things up as we went."

At the time, Ammons had a programming background and had managed software development projects before. He knew quick wins to implement, like how to improve "obvious things" like team onboarding and process.

Ammons credits his willingness to "step into the fire" and solve hard problems while teaching others how to perform instead of doing the work himself with his advancement. "I got promoted into a CTO role, and I moved away from writing code every day and more into making sure, as the team grew, that it was high functioning, working well with design and product."

Ammons says, looking back, that they didn't have all of the answers, but he was always clear on wanting the team to be successful and build things that were valuable to users. To elevate his skills as he stepped into the c-suite, he consumed educational materials from other developers, followed other companies, and implemented systems like agile software development.

Ammons says his first executive role was as a "tactical CTO" focused on how they hire people and get them working on areas that solve problems for customers. He says if he were to do the role again, he'd have focused on delivering to the company.

"I'd probably be more involved in understanding the business side of things and making sure that rather than solving things efficiently, they were solving the right things that would lead to revenue growth and customer expansion.

"In my own company I founded after I left that first job, we built a bunch of stuff that we didn't end up actually needing and spent way too much time on things that didn't matter," says Ammons.

LEARNING TO LET GO OF BEING THE ONE TO WRITE CODE AND SHIFTING TO EMPOWERING HIS TEAM

Ammons says he's had to let go of writing and even reviewing code now that he's an engineering leader. His advice for new engineering executives is to shift from doing things themselves to learning to build tools and systems that enable developers to work better.

"I'm no longer a good developer because I am not spending eight hours a day doing it now that I'm a startup leader," says Ammons. "I'm not the best person to be doing code reviews or giving anyone feedback on their code. Effectiveness is now all about empowering my team to contribute," says Ammons.

ON INTERNAL PROMOTIONS: NICK MEHTA'S PERSPECTIVE AS CEO OF GAINSIGHT

Internal promotions come with the upside of people already aligned with company values and "hungry" to win promotion. They signal positively to the rest of the team that they could get promoted too. Candidates from within may not be as experienced as others on the leadership team. Those on the "outside" may not perceive them to be experienced and thus that leader may struggle with hiring based on their professional brand.

Why? Because people often are more hesitant to work for a first-time leader. They know that the first-time leader probably isn't "tested" in the same way a multi-company executive would be. Remember, when you're hiring a team, they're betting on your ability to lead them well as much as you're betting on them to perform for your organization.

"If I have super talented leaders that are early in their career and got promoted internally, nobody will work for them from the outside because they look them up on LinkedIn and say, oh my gosh, this person is brand new to this job," says Mehta.

To overcome this situation, you need to get around that bias and become a great talent recruiter. Figure out ways you can position your value as the servant–leader to future hires. Sell potential candidates on how focused you'll be on helping them quickly acclimatize to the company culture, and how you'll help them achieve their own career growth (like you). Help them see the work you've already done (and will continue doing) to be a mature, stable, and respectful boss who is there for them and their career success. Don't try to hide reality; speak to it directly, confidently, and show what you'd bring to them and why you're excited about them, specifically, joining and becoming a part of your organization.

Make the story about them and shift the focus from you and your tenure, and you'll win a lot of points. This is another reason why having a strong peer network matters. If you are awesome to work with and past colleagues want to join you, that's going to set you up down the road. As you're navigating an internal promotion, you can then confidently share how you'll build your team from the talent network around you, and that can help you get the job.

GETTING HIRED: LANDING THE ROLE

The co-founder or c-level executive who's hiring you is making the decision based on your ability to own a function and prove you can build and scale the organization. They're evaluating your fit with the startup stage as much as you are evaluating them.

What's on a CEO or co-founder's mind when thinking about hiring externally vs. internally:

External candidates:

- Risk of unknown.
- More work and expense to recruit them.

- Time to value higher vs. internal (could they produce meaningful results in < 90 days? Probably not).
- Often higher compensation expectations.
- Brings in new perspectives and experience.
- The grass is greener (he was at another Unicorn so he must be a genius).
- Looks better to board members.

Internal candidates:

- Lower risk of being a total miss (they know the weaknesses already).
- Faster ramp-up time.
- Likely have to replace a strong individual contributor when moving internal candidate out.
- Board may see as a risk vs. hiring a proven expert.
- Knows a lot about the business but may not know a lot about the role.
- Cultural impacts and incentives.

If you're an external candidate, you can look for a startup that fits your profile in the following ways:

- Look for job posts on LinkedIn that list "head of" roles in your desired startup stage and market.
- Reach out to industry groups like Pavilion for job posts and/or affinity groups like Lesbians Who Tech, People of Color in Tech, Girls Who Code, and other organizations, which can be especially useful to get a foot in the door at a place you'd like to join as a member of an underrepresented minority.
- Contact former bosses and/or industry contacts to see if they're hiring; sometimes your former counterparts have leveled up and will be able to see you as a leveled-up person too.
- Work on your CV to map the skills and background you've got already to the role you want (think about ownership).
- Think about stories that tell the role you played in being a high performer at your last role—convince the team that you know how the recipe to make the new startup as successful as the big company or the startup you were at before without the official executive title.

- Reach out to a former boss who's co-founded a smaller venture and would be willing to take a bet on you in your first leadership role due to knowing and trusting you to perform above your previous rank.

Sometimes, you have to leave your current organization to get noticed as the executive you're ready to become. It can be hard to be at a place with a leader in the role where you know you could do the job but that opening just isn't there. While you're looking for your next startup role externally, you shouldn't discount the potential of being promoted at your current organization. We'll tackle that in the next chapter.

INTERNAL PROMOTIONS TO EXECUTIVE ARE POSSIBLE, BUT NOT AT EVERY COMPANY

By understanding the skills your function requires, whether that be on the go-to-market or product side of the business, you'll be positioned to prove you're ready for the role.

"Make it really easy for the overworked CEO to just accept that this has really already happened," says startup executive Matt Harada.

Advocate for making the leap by recruiting mentors and chipping away at your list of the skills and experiences you want to gain as you ascend into leadership ranks. If your company won't promote you, but you've done everything you can to become the type of leader who's promotable, you'll have a greater chance of landing that first executive seat elsewhere.

CHAPTER FIVE

Get the Offer and Secure Your Executive Seat

You've found the right company, the right stage, and you've started to interview, or you're in the process of negotiating a promotion at your current company. How do you actually secure the role?

Whether you're accepting a role at your existing company or a new venture, successfully navigating the offer stage is a critical area of startup joiner life. A full discussion about the ins and outs of startup employee contracts is out of the scope of this book, but we'll cover a few of the main process points from a long-term success standpoint, to help you make the most of your pre-joining experience. This section is about helping you make the case for yourself for transitioning into your first startup executive role.

FIND YOUR FIRST (OR NEXT) EXECUTIVE ROLE

Look on LinkedIn, Glassdoor, or in an industry group channel like Pavilion. There are groups dedicated to executive roles. Ask your peers. Look at the fundraising in newsletters like StrictlyVC or MorningBrew. You can see which stage companies have raised, and often, they'll be ready to bring on new leaders. (You can always do a cold outreach.)

INTERVIEWING FOR YOUR EXECUTIVE ROLE

If you're aiming for a promotion within your organization, your interview process for your promotion to executive level may be as simple as a discussion with your C-level boss. But if you're applying to join an external startup, they'll have various stages of maturity in their HR/People Ops program, and you can expect to go through a multi-stage, sometimes laborious, hiring process.

NAVIGATING THE OFTEN BYZANTINE STARTUP HIRING PROCESS

Remember that startups, like you, are looking for alignment in their senior leadership. They are interested in finding out how the person they bring aboard will complement the current leadership team in skills and experience, as well as bring new perspectives that will enrich the business and help it grow. They want to feel confident that this person can grow and lead a team, can be held accountable for results, and steward their function successfully.

THE INTERVIEW PROCESS

Your mileage may vary, and startups tend to do this differently and change as they grow, but, in general, you can expect to meet a hiring manager, then usually the founder/CEO, then other teams, then a presentation about your 30–60–90 plan for your function. That's fairly typical, and involves some work at each stage to learn more about the company and for them to learn more about you.

Depending on your function, you can reference examples of other presentations online, but be sure to tailor yours to what you've learned about the business. Feel free to also reference the QBR section of this book in the "reporting your results" chapter to help you tell the story of what success will look like. (This positions you well when you go and make it happen as a member of the team, and then need to report actual results in a QBR!)

UNDERSTAND THE PRESENTATION TECH STACK AND PRACTICE YOUR PRESENTATION WITH FRIENDS

Familiarize yourself with the software you'll be presenting (such as on Zoom or Hangouts), assuming this is a remote role or interview. If in-person, figure out what tech stack you'll be using to present to the hiring company. Imagine this as a leadership team meeting where you're talking about your vision, confidently sharing your approach, as well as showing that you've learned enough about the startup to dig in and start making an impact in the first few weeks on the job. If you're nervous about presenting, practice with a friend.

MEETING WITH THE CEO: UNDERSTAND THEIR VISION

As a joiner, particularly at the leadership level, you need to believe in the CEO's ability to lead successfully. This person is flying the proverbial rocket ship as you're going to be building it. Often, the CEO will be one of your first and last interviews. The CEO can go into "sell mode" and try to entice you to join as a senior leader, and they also can sniff out any misalignments as they have more context and visibility than anyone else in the organization.

Things you can ask a CEO or a founder during your interview that will help you get a true grip on the business financials, mission, and culture:

- What's your perspective on our business growth over the next 6–12 months and the role my function (and I) will play in this growth?
- How big is our total addressable market (TAM) and how will we ensure we're growing fast enough to compete successfully in the market we're disrupting?
- What's something a leader you work with would say about how to work well with you?
- When someone doesn't know something, how do we incentivize learning in a safe way so we can incorporate those insights to move faster?
- When have you managed someone who wasn't as strong in a particular area or had a misstep and how did they overcome it (or, have you ever been that person?). (This question matters because startups are all about experimentation, learning, and incorporating those insights quickly to scale results. If you're entering an environment where people are expected to be perfect, and know everything all the time, and never mess up, perhaps due to the unhealthy pressure the founders put on themselves at the top, you should know about it! Every time I've explored this question upfront either by asking it or experiencing the first evidence of how the company deals with it firsthand, it has always had a profound impact on my happiness at a company long-term. This is something that is so baked into the culture of a company that once you know the truth about it, you have to decide if you're okay with it or not. Don't expect it to change.)

- How essential is (my function) to the organization's goals? It's especially nice to ask this if you think it's important, and want to remind them and get on the same page about how much value you'll bring when you come in and crush it. Alternatively, sometimes the answer will totally shock you like, "actually I don't think we really need sales, this product sells itself," and as a prospective VP of Sales, you should know this.
- Thoughts on going upmarket or downmarket? Are we selling to the right customers?
- What's your vision for fundraising in the near and long term? Any thoughts on an exit and/or are you thinking to grow the business through IPO, acquisition? (Note: all of this can change five minutes after you talk to the CEO, but it can be helpful to hear where their head is at the time of your joining).
- What do the company values mean to you? Is there a particular value that has come from your own life experience or other founders' experiences? At any healthy company, a founder will create values that are shaped by the need to mitigate against unhealthy past experiences and behaviors. This is what values are all about; taking a stand on something. For instance, "talk straight," a value at ServiceRocket, meant that people would speak openly about what was on their minds without being political or going to another party. Direct, open communication was a value, and it was shaped by the founder's strong commitment to healthy dialogue and relationships. If your company doesn't yet have values, you can ask a founder to talk about something they do at work that has been shaped by past experiences.
- What kinds of things are you into outside of work? Any fun hobbies? This is up to you, but being relationship-oriented can be a very good thing early on, and sometimes it'll help to make a concerted effort to get to know this person whom you'll spend a lot of time talking to, reporting to, following, and learning from (and teaching!). It's also a chance to disclose any non-visible differences (per your comfort level) to see if they will be tolerated or, ideally, embraced. For example, I come out as LGBTQ+ during the interview process prior to joining a startup. It's a huge privilege to be able to, as I know many can't, depending on geography and other circumstances. I do because I can choose not to work for companies where it would be an issue. I sleep better at night knowing I won't have to hide a big part of my identity at work.

WHEN THE STARTUP'S HIRING PROCESS GOES AWRY

An early-stage startup's disorganized hiring process can be jarring on the candidate's side, to the degree that it's worth discussing. Depending on the stage you're joining, People Ops may not be fully built out, so your mileage with the hiring experience may not be ideal. For example, you could have multiple meandering multi-hour conversations with a founder without the sense that there's a clear hiring framework for the role. If you can, push back on any lack of structure with your own boundaries and timelines, so you're not stuck doing consulting for free.

Alternatively, you deserve a timely response. If you don't hear back for ages, feel free to inquire. Many startups don't take the step of disqualifying candidates and letting them know. Instead, they just disqualify or "DQ" them in their applicant tracking system (ATS). Ghosting does happen, but thankfully it's becoming less standard.

Anything that's wonky about your startup hiring experience won't necessarily be a reflection of the overall startup experience. Perhaps the People Ops program is under-resourced. For example, if a calendar invite is added incorrectly during your interview process, don't take it as a sign that the entire company is a dumpster fire. (At a later-stage company, you could potentially extrapolate that. The hiring process should have matured alongside the business. Note: this is referring to organizational challenges or disorganization in the hiring experience.) If you experience bias or anything discriminatory in the interview process, listen to your inner voice. Those factors could become baked into the company culture, unlike calendar invite whiffs, which likely will improve as the company grows.

I have never regretted listening to my weird spidey senses early in the interview process at a startup. I once received a startup leadership offer at a company that had very bad Glassdoor reviews from women alleging discriminatory, sexist behavior at the company in one particular department (not the one I was planning on joining), with particular call-outs to the behavior of the CEO in reinforcing the alleged issues. Because I liked other aspects of the role and the company had a great reputation in the market, I decided to gather more data before making a decision. I brought these reviews up with the CEO during the interview process, hoping he would express some concern for the content raised in them and ideally a concrete plan for addressing the discrimination allegations from past employees.

Instead, he had the gall to ask me to help him reply to the comments on his behalf—for free, before getting hired. For context, I was interviewing for a revenue marketing role that was tasked with increasing market share, not PR or HR (not that it would have been appropriate if I'd been going for one of those roles either). It didn't seem to occur to him that maybe *he* should be the one to review the comments and take the feedback seriously. I don't think he realized these allegations themselves were something that would potentially prevent me from taking the job; he was mostly concerned about me solving this issue for him once it came to his attention rather than dealing with the issue itself! Needless to say, I did not take the job offer.

Trust your judgment; if something feels off, and not just disorganized, find out what's underneath your gut reaction. At the least, you'll know if you leaped to conclusions too early based on false assumptions or incorrect pattern matching. Doing more research will help you see exactly why this organization is or isn't a good environment for you.

GETTING THE OFFER

Congrats, you found a company you like, and they've made an offer to bring you aboard as a leader! At this point, you think the leadership team is smart and capable (and the CEO highly capable). Now you're ready to get your offer. Note that format matters, even in remote-first roles; it's best to discuss compensation expectations early and over the phone/Zoom instead of in writing. Most businesses are not legally allowed to ask you what you made in previous roles, but they will expect you to give them a range. Ideally, there's an HR team to go over this with you, but, if not, your CEO/co-founder will take on that role.

Note: if you give a range and increase it later in the process, that can cause frustration for the hiring team, so make sure you're truly comfortable with the range. Alternatively, you can ask the startup to tell you the range they're expecting to pay for the role, and research to see if you're in the ballpark for your geography and region. Particularly around equity vs. cash, it can be challenging to know the value of equity until you understand more about the business metrics, so a good frame would be to shoot for "on target earnings" or "OTE" and have the exact breakdown of cash (base/bonus) plus equity and benefits in mind going into discussions. Startup executives tend to have a higher percentage of compensation with equity and bonus than ICs or mid-level managers. You may be used to a higher base and less variable compensation, so, in this chapter, we'll cover some of the considerations.

Negotiations happen best face-to-face, on calls, or over Zoom. Try not to negotiate in writing; it's harder to get the crucial feedback in real-time you need to effectively learn what counts to the startup (and for them to learn what's important to you) if you're not doing it in real-time.

COMPENSATION BREAKDOWN

All compensation (comp) plans at startups include a variety of elements that roll up to your "total compensation." Things like "on target earnings" or OTE are expressions that explain the sum of the parts you'll receive in your offer. Typically, startups will offer you a few options to choose from that include more equity vs. cash or vice versa. More startups are publishing salary bands—in some areas, it's even required to include this in job postings. Most are working on overcoming bias in the negotiation process. If you're given the option to choose a heavier cash or equity offer, you'll need to prioritize.

In *Ask For More: 10 Questions To Negotiate Anything*, author Alexandra Carter, Director of the Columbia Law School Mediation Clinic, explains that any negotiation, even financial or for an offer letter, involves our "love and belonging" needs.

Carter suggests that while "concrete needs" from salary negotiations are undoubtedly involved, "intangible" needs are also at play when we negotiate for our compensation in a new job. "In my experience, people often ask . . . for money because they can't contract for love, appreciation, or acceptance."[1] Carter says that identifying our concrete needs (how much comp do I need for financial obligations) and less concrete needs like recognition, reputation, and appreciation (being paid market rate for your role, being demonstratively valued by your employer, etc.) are crucial.

By following Carter's advice on asking ourselves what's really important to us and why, we can verify that we're negotiating for the right things, for the right reason, while being open to what's valued by others (in this case, your new startup).

NEGOTIATING THE OFFER

Before we can truly listen to and understand someone else's side of the things when negotiating any kind of deal, we have to truly understand our own.[2]

We must also understand our feelings. Carter says, "If your negotiation involves people (i.e. you), it's personal, and feelings will be part of it."[3] Carter suggests the following tips for negotiation, including considering prior success, listening to what the other side is concerned about, and asking what the other side needs.

DO YOUR RESEARCH

Executive compensation is a moving target and every year the benchmarks change. Research in industry forums like Pavillion, Glassdoor, and other industry resources indicate what's standard for your level and geography, stage company, and experience.

RISK VS. REWARD: A NOTE ABOUT EQUITY

Equity is a complex topic and deserves expert attention. Equity is by no means guaranteed income, yet is often a significant part of your overall comp as a leader at a startup. It doesn't matter if you negotiate 0.75% or 0.5% if your company never has any liquidity event or fails, but if your company eventually becomes worth $20 billion, well, it matters a lot. That's part of the risk/reward tradeoff for joining a company early-stage vs. later. There's a clearer sense of what your equity will be worth.

According to *The Holloway Guide to Equity Compensation*, "For companies whose stock prices have appreciated significantly, the out-of-pocket amounts can be huge and thus prohibitively expensive for many employees. In some ways, it's a success disaster—that is, employees are penalized for actually succeeding in building a business that is now worth so much (thus they can't afford to exercise their options). This undermines the cash–equity trade-off that many startup employees make."[4]

If you're new to receiving equity as a part of your total compensation, or perhaps have never received a significant amount, this chapter can help guide you to understand the concepts at a broad level and point you to other resources to inform your choices. Please note that nothing in this chapter should serve as legal nor tax advice. Seek professional advice for any individual guidance.

FIND OUT THE PERCENTAGE OF EQUITY BEING RECEIVED AND ITS CURRENT VALUE

Receiving thousands of shares may sound like a lot, but it's important to find out what percentage of the total shares this represents, as well as their current value. Startup executives tend to receive higher stock option grants than other employees, and you can research the norms for your particular role and startup stage in industry groups.

Ideally, the CEO and/or CFO should have some idea of how many option receiving positions the company needs and plan out the percentage for each level accordingly. At many startups, employees in the same level should get the same percent, but not all startups do that, because some employees have more leverage or are better negotiators.

According to Matt Harada, if the company has thoughtfully planned out bands and has consistent percentages for each band, equity offers become easier for both the startup and the employee.

If that is the case, and the VP option level is only 0.2%, it may be because the company is planning on needing a big team to hit its $1 billion valuation and needs to slice the pie pretty thin to hire the number of VPs it needs. But it will be a big pie.

The right number depends on so many things that are knowable: the odds that the company will ever get an exit (sale or IPO), what value will that be, how much dilution will happen from future rounds of financing. Getting 0.5% vs. 0.25% is great, but if this is a company that you truly believe could be a $1 billion unicorn, 0.25% is still pretty life-changing and way better than 0.5% of a company that fails. Knowing the percentage is an important first step. From there it gets difficult. The variability will be large depending on the stage of the company and expectations for future equity transactions (dilutive funding rounds and how close to an exit the company is).

Sample Option Pool Plan By Startup CEO Matt Harada

Example 1				
	Headcount By Level			
Department	**C-Level**	**VP**	**Dir**	**Total**
Sales	1	1	3	
Marketing		1	1	
Account Management		1	2	
Engineer	1	1	3	
Product		1	2	
Operations		1	2	
Finance/HR	1	-	2	
Total Headcount	3	6	15	24
% Per Head	2.50%	0.50%	0.10%	
Total	7.50%	3.00%	1.50%	**12.00%**
Example Exit				
Common Value At Option Grant	$5,000,000			
Value Available To Common	$200,000,000			
Fully Vested Value Per Head	**$4,875,000**	**$975,000**	**$195,000**	

Example 2				
	Headcount By Level			
Department	**C-Level**	**VP**	**Dir**	**Total**
Sales	1	3	6	
Marketing		2	2	
Account Management		2	4	
Engineer	1	3	6	
Product		2	4	
Operations		3	4	
Finance/HR	1	2	4	
Total Headcount	3	17	30	50
% Per Head	2.00%	0.25%	0.05%	
Total	6.00%	4.25%	1.50%	**11.75%**
Example Exit				
Common Value At Option Grant	$10,000,000			
Value Available To Common	$1,000,000,000			
Fully Vested Value Per Head	**$19,800,000**	**$2,475,000**	**$495,000**	

UNDERSTAND YOUR VESTING SCHEDULE IN YOUR OFFER

The typical vesting schedule for startup equity is around four years, with a one-year cliff (the minimum period of time you'll need to be on board before your shares vest). As Scott Kupor points out in *Secrets of Sand Hill Road*, startups don't necessarily go public in four years. (It's more common to take longer these days, which is another topic entirely.) Understand how long you'll need to stay at the company to vest your equity and whether there would be an acceleration of your equity in a liquidity event.

FIND OUT THE TAX IMPLICATIONS OF YOUR EQUITY

All startup leaders with "skin in the game" (equity compensation, in startup speak) need to assess the tax implications of their equity and how they'll navigate them. While this section includes neither legal nor tax advice, it should point you in the right direction to make informed choices.

Equities are an asset class, like real estate or bonds. Like other asset classes, equity is subject to taxation in the United States. When and how you can pay the least taxes on it depends on a number of factors. Accredited accountants or financial advisors can help you assess your individual tax situation and the best choices based on your needs. There are some scenarios in which people choose to pay taxes early on equity, even prior to vesting, which comes with its own complications.

At a high level, the tax implications are dependent on factors that include:

- Your personal financial and tax liability situation.
- How much the shares are worth (the "fair market value" or "FMV") when your equity options are issued to you, how early the company is (seed round, series A, series B, etc.), and how much you estimate they will be worth at a liquidity event (i.e., Initial Public Offering, acquisition). This difference between what shares are worth when issued to you and what they're worth during a liquidity event is known as the "spread." Note: this is very hard to estimate, but an accountant can run you through some scenarios and what tax implications would be to pay taxes early based on the current value.
- Exercising options once shares vest starts what's known as the "capital gains clock" so you'd be paying ideally a smaller amount than after the shares soar. That's part of the gamble of choosing to exercise your vested startup options prior to a liquidity event (when the value is determined and you're able to turn the shares into cold hard cash), because remember, this may all become worthless. Hopefully not, but you can't count on them.
- Your financial situation and whether you can afford to pay the taxes early.

HIRE AN ACCOUNTANT AS SOON AS YOU ACCEPT AN OFFER

You'll want to check in with your accountant *as soon as you accept your startup job offer*. There is a time window when you can make certain tax decisions. Plan to have a timely conversation with a trusted accountant and/or financial advisor. Some questions to ask:

- Would it benefit you personally to file an 83B and/or pay taxes early based on how well you think the company could do vs. the downside if they failed and the equity became worth nothing or if a liquidity event took a long time?
- When you vest your equity (again, usually after a one-year cliff), should you exercise your shares early based on the financials of the company and your personal financials?
- Can you afford to potentially lose all of the money you spend on taxes and/or your equity or wait a long time? For example, I've exercised shares at a profitable self-funded company that probably won't take VC pressure to have a liquidity event any time soon, and they're not ready to IPO. Barring another liquidity scenario, I had to be comfortable with the equity that had been vested and I'd exercised potentially staying just there: shares sitting in my account.

Some great resources to learn more about equity and taxes:

- Check out Carta, an equity platform commonly used by startups.
- *The Holloway Guide to Equity Compensation* by Joshua Levy, Joe Wallin, Dmitriy Kharchenko, and Hope Hackett.

A NOTE ON EARLY-STAGE EQUITY

Early-stage equity shows alignment with incentives. If you want too much cash early, it can scare founders—remember, they're taking a big salary cut. Your startup may likely have equity that's worth little to nothing, so be clear about the risk you're taking and ensure that it aligns with your total compensation expectations and needs.

HIRE A LAWYER TO REVIEW YOUR OFFER LETTER AND CONTRACT

A legal review is worthwhile for *any* work contract you sign, but especially at the executive level. A great lawyer can be more affordable than you think. Often lawyers will agree to do "package deals" on your negotiation deals, so they're not billing you endless hours working on your contract before you've even signed the thing that nets income. Note: you may resist hiring a lawyer for your contract through fear of spending money on something before you've earned any from it. That mindset can hurt you down the road. Investing early in creating a great contract pays dividends in many scenarios.

If you hire a lawyer to review your contract, companies won't (or shouldn't) take it as a sign of lack of enthusiasm about the job. At that point, you're excited about them, they're excited about you. You can bet your startup has hired a lawyer to review all of their documents. It's a sign of maturity and self-advocacy that you bring on counsel to help you negotiate for what matters to you in your offer and the terms agreed upon work for you (and your startup).

Ask around your local business chamber, network, and/or Google local law-yers who specifically specialize in helping startup employees. Note: if you don't hire a lawyer to look over your contracts, at the least, read it very, very carefully yourself. Lawyers can protect your own intellectual property, include language that adds in exit packages, clarify non-competes, and can even help you include additional terms that matter to you.

Sometimes you can even ask your startup to pay for it or split the costs. You're worth it and once you're at the offer stage, it benefits them to do what it takes to close you as a candidate.

NEGOTIATING YOUR TITLE

The "head of role" is a nebulous catch-all that startups often use when they're uncertain how to position someone or to make room to hire over them in a start-up's early days and to avoid inflation. It can be interpreted as Director and VP, and can sometimes even mean C-level. What's most significant about the title is the possibility for overseeing the entire department and moving into a true execu-tive position.

If this is your first startup leadership role and/or depending on the stage and maturity of your company, you may likely be offered "head of" in your title. If this is the case, clarify what "head of" means in terms of leveling at your current company. If you're brought in as "head of," does that mean you're a director-level or C-level? For instance, at Asana, "Head of" applies to C-level, but most startups define C-level, VP, Director, and so forth as they scale. "Head of" is merely a place-holder until they build out that leveling.

If your CEO is willing to bring you on as a VP or C-level, go for it! If they insist you take the "head of" title until later, you can ask to get it written into your contract to renegotiate the title at a certain date (for example, six months in, or at a key fundraising event). Depending on your experience level, leaders can "level up" by coming in at a "head of" title and then proving their success and going for the official promotion.

CASH VS. EQUITY: FOOD FOR THOUGHT

Early-stage startups often need to conserve cash, so it benefits them to offer employees longer-term incentives like more equity or negotiating for higher cash upon business milestones like fundraising rounds. Carter advocates asking ourselves and the other party "what would fairness look like for you here?" and sharing as much knowledge and data so we can creatively come to agreements together. In a startup salary negotiation, you can ask for information from the startup-like "when do we plan on raising another round of funding?" and "what's our cash position right now?" and "what's our capitalization table (analysis of the company's percentage of ownership and equity breakdown) look like?"

Come to the negotiation prepared with objective data on market compensation for your position based on industry research and talking with peers at other organizations. Although startups People/HR teams may do this research in advance, you'll want to do your own due diligence. Sometimes startups have bands for employees and offer employees several choices to choose from—some higher cash, some higher equity. Startups are also increasingly offering transparency in their salary banding.

Once during a compensation negotiation, I made assumptions about the cap table and didn't ask for more equity, because I didn't think it was available for my role given how much equity I already had compared to industry benchmarks. I didn't think asking for more equity was even possible.

Instead of assuming, I should have asked to verify our equity situation if it mattered to me. (It did!) The founder, who was thoughtful, said "If you'd like to talk about increasing your compensation partly via more equity, would you like to better understand our cap table and have visibility?" This led to a wonderful, informative discussion about not only our capitalization but also about his excitement about incentivizing me long-term in the business and growing my company ownership options.

Our discussion included his vision for how our business would grow and raise funds over the coming 18 months. It was great that he thought to tell me all of this and speaks volumes about his leadership. In the future, I'd ask upfront if in doubt. The worst that would have happened would have been the founder saying he couldn't share the information. It never hurts to ask for the information you want in a negotiation, as long as you're asking in a respectful way. Startup founders are here to create exciting offers for their leadership teams to incentivize them to align with the growth of the business. Let them help you help them make you the best offer possible! If in doubt: consult a compensation expert.

MORE ON EQUITY AND CAP TABLES FOR UNDER-REPRESENTED STARTUP LEADERS

The percentage of the cap table owned by under-represented minorities is still abysmal in 2022, at the time of publishing. No matter your startup stage, we owe it to ourselves to advocate for equity. Women own just 9% of startup equity.[5]

At times in the business, you'll be able to get more cash, like at certain growth milestones or at a fundraising event.

"One of the biggest things I tell everyone is this: You're deserving, and you don't get what you don't ask for. If asking for what you're worth is uncomfortable, why is that? You should try to shift your mindset because your counterparts are having those conversations," says marketing executive Rachel Beisel.

A WORD: IF THE DEAL GOES SOUTH WHILE YOU'RE IN NEGOTIATIONS

This is a section that almost didn't seem necessary until conversations with other leaders and remembering with less rosy lenses made me reflect on my past experiences. Sometimes, not often, you'll be doing a deal for a job and be right at the finish line and it won't work out. Sometimes, a deal just doesn't go the way you want, and you don't know until it's late in the negotiation or offer stage. It hurts to have that happen after you've put a lot of work into the offer process, but it's better to advocate for your needs than signing something that will make you and the company unhappy in the short or long term.

AFTER YOU SIGN THE DEAL

Celebrate! You've earned it. Go for a hike, hug a dog, take your kids to a baseball game, read a fun book and go to bed early, toast a glass of cava on a rooftop in Barcelona. Whatever you do, be sure to bask in the glory of your achievement.

PART II

GETTING STARTED: NAIL YOUR FIRST 90 DAYS

CHAPTER SIX

Define Your Goals and Align with Your CEO and Board on Success

Congratulations, you've got the job—now the fun part begins. It's time to create your success plan for crushing it in your first 90 days on the job.

Y ou're in your leadership role and you're ready to get started. Whether you're a seasoned startup leader or in a first-time leadership role, every new "at bat" requires us to prepare for the task at hand: namely, setting up our first 90 days for success. Many startups require leadership candidates to present their 90-day plan during the interview process. If you've made one of these, that's a great step. Even so, you'll still likely need to completely overhaul it once you join the company and see all the fun stuff under the hood that you had no idea was there! I've heard this referred to by a startup founder as "finding out where the bodies are buried."

Before we get into how to build your 90-day plan, set goals, and work with your CEO, board, executive team, and reports to be successful, let's talk about the purpose of your first 90 days. It might seem obvious to some—if you're on a quarterly system, you should probably measure effectiveness in the first quarter for a new startup leader. Still, it's useful to unpack the logic for getting an executive ramped (and ramping yourself!) out of the gate.

YOUR FIRST 90 DAYS: ONBOARDING TO YOUR NEW ROLE AND PROVING YOUR VALUE TO THE ORGANIZATION

Too few startup joiners give enough attention to succeeding in their first term. This period is the make-or-break for most leadership roles. To earn a seat, many joiners are required to present their first 90-day plans. Companies want to know that a startup leader can quickly onboard, understand the business objectives, and align their program for driving the overall organization's success.

Your first days at your company will set the tone for whether or not you succeed in your role. If you are not successful in this time period, you will be let go.

When I look back at the first 90-day plan I created for my most recent executive role, as well as the 90-day Quarterly Business Review (QBR) presentation I delivered, reporting on this time period after it transpired, I see that *so* much of what we've done over the past several years in our organization started with the seeds of what was uncovered and built in that tender early time period. Many of the problems we uncovered were solvable, and proving early wins during this time solidified my position in the role and gave me and the company confidence beyond that initial period.

DON'T BE SHY ABOUT MAKING AN IMPACT RIGHT AWAY

One pitfall to avoid in your first 90 days is thinking that you need to "play nice" or sit back and spend too long "learning and digging in." This is especially common when you are taking on your first startup leadership role and you've come from a larger company and don't want to ruffle feathers. While a lot will be wrong with your startup and you won't want to go in too aggressively before understanding, once you have context, it's your job to improve things and build upon what's already there. If you can't make an impact in the first 90 days, people will doubt you ever will (whether or not that's true).

Remember that your CEO and board hired or promoted you because they trust you to have discernment, and to use your skills and experience to share an honest assessment of what's going well and what's not in your department and the business, as well as how you've learned from any mistakes you've made or issues you've uncovered. You're on board to shake things up and make things better, so don't be afraid to take some risks and learn from them, as well as take actions that will put points on the board.

Once, I worked with a sales executive with whom everyone liked and enjoyed being with in meetings. But around 60 days, it was clear he couldn't point to any contributions or strong positions on anything we'd done prior to him joining. He stayed too long in "learning" mode and didn't take enough meaningful actions to move the business forward. There is no room at the executive level for benevolent observers. Startups can't afford executives who wait and learn for too long; they need leaders who run experiments and learn quickly so they can improve and then run better tests in the future. His inability to make a measurable change in the business in any area cost him the role. (As an aside, he ended up leaving just shy of the 90-day milestone.)

As Matt Heinz, co-founder of CMO Coffee Talk, a worldwide community for chief marketing officers, says when it comes to startup executives, "no one hires you to sail a smooth sailing ship."

"In my experience, the board does not expect us to have all the answers all the time, but rather to see that we are on top of the gaps and actively seeking solutions," said Heinz. "A sense of curiosity and urgency too."

In mythology, a hero's origin story sets the tone for their great journey. Your first 90 days is the origin of YOUR hero story at your company. Ready to don a cape? Here's what to expect in your successful first 90 days:

- Build relationships with key stakeholders at the company, including your peers on the leadership team, your CEO, and cross-functional teams, as well as any inherited reports.
- Audit and understand the current state of the business and your department/area: what's working in the business? Where are things already going well?
- Learn what's broken, not working: areas in the business that are on fire that you're actively working on, or will be soon.
- Assess the business objectives for the next quarter, half, and year (and beyond) and how your organization will impact those.
- Assess the team structure and hiring plan. Who's going to be in your organization, and how will this headcount tie back to hitting your business objectives?
- Set up a regular 1:1 cadence with your CEO, peers, and team. Onboarding to my leadership role, my CEO and I met once a week at the top of the week, once at the end of the week (a wrap-up), and once every other week in the middle for a 1:1 outside of just business topics (relationship-based). This was absolutely crucial for our alignment and communication success, especially during the early days of the pandemic, when we were doing my onboarding all remotely.

GET POINTS ON THE BOARD EARLY BY FOCUSING ON ACCOMPLISHING SEVERAL LOW EFFORT, HIGH IMPACT INITIATIVES IN YOUR FIRST 90 DAYS

When Gainsight CEO Nick Mehta hired a new head of corporate development strategy, that person set a goal of meeting 50 customers in the first 90 days.

"Setting an ambitious goal right away sends a signal that you're serious and you're going to get things done," says Mehta.

Mehta recommends bucketing the "wins" in the first 90 days into four categories:

- Small impact, low effort (postpone most, do a few of them).
- Small impact, big effort (avoid).
- Big impact, low effort (do as many of these as you can!).
- Big impact, big effort (postpone most, do a few of them).

Nick Mehta says that after meeting with stakeholders and employees, you'll understand the kinds of challenges the organization is facing. During your first 30 days, you can knock out some easy wins that will win the hearts and minds of your colleagues.

"Do something very specific and easy to fix and it makes them feel like you have a bias to action," says Mehta.

Do a few important things in the first 90 days that people care about and get excited about and make an impact quickly. Never underestimate the power of solving other people's problems that are easy for you to fix and make a big difference in their work lives! If you wait to solve one big problem at the end of 90 days, you're missing an opportunity to make a great impression and do some good right away.

WORK WITH YOUR CEO TO IDENTIFY SUCCESS

Chris Motley, founder, and CEO of Mentor Spaces, works with his leaders to help them understand what success looks like specifically for them.

"We as founders can talk about what success looks like for the business with our eyes closed and hands tied behind our backs," says Motley. "But at the end of the day, the leaders on our teams are executing the growth strategy, and it is important to articulate what success looks like for them, individually and within their specific role," says Motley.

Motley says he advises his leaders to understand and communicate how to add value at the specific stage of growth, knowing that they may have more knowledge than the founder at any point on how they can be successful in their role.

"If the founder knew how to perform certain roles at a high level, they probably wouldn't hire that person in the first place," says Motley.

Motley tells his executive team to think like advisors to the founders and to share their plan for how their department will help the founder achieve the company vision.

"I coach my leadership team to understand my role, which is to not run out of money, hire great people, and constantly reinforce the vision. I also help them to understand their role, which is to make our customers and users successful, communicate a rolling 30–60–90-day plan on how they will accomplish that, and align on accountability metrics that lets everyone know if we're on track or not," says Motley.

"ARE WE SEEING THE SAME GAME?"

Famed American football coach Bill Parcells would watch his quarterback, Phil Simms, making decisions on the field that Parcells did not agree with. When Phil came off the field, Parcells would say to him, "Are we seeing the same game?"

meaning, "this is what I see and what I think you should be doing. What are you seeing that is causing you to make the choices you are making?"

Organizational psychologist and executive coach Dennis Adsit notes that startup leaders can often find themselves in conflict with their CEOs. This is because many startup leaders have different perceptions than their CEOs about what's happening in a given situation. If this is the case, Adsit recommends that they work to make sure everyone is "seeing the same game" and align on the current reality and the best course of action.

This is best accomplished by alternating statements with questions. The leader could say to the CEO, "This is how I am seeing Current Reality, including the internal Strengths and Weaknesses and external Opportunities, Threats (also known as SWOT). Is that how you see it?"

If there is alignment, move on to describe the recommended course of action for progressing or closing a key gap and share your logic for that choice. Adsit recommends following that with a question: "I am curious if you see gaps in my thinking and if therefore you think we should be doing something else?"

This is a robust approach for getting aligned with any key stakeholder with whom there is a conflict about how to proceed.

ADVICE FROM A CEO TO STARTUP EXECUTIVES: REMEMBER THAT THE CEO ROLE IS TOUGH

Especially during the pandemic, many CEOs have been under tremendous pressure to deliver business results while dealing with a global crisis on multiple fronts. Heavy is the head that wears the crown. When your CEO makes a mistake or does something you wouldn't have done, remember that we are all human and CEOs are under tremendous pressure. After all, wouldn't you want them to extend the same empathy to you?

"Anyone who willingly takes on the role of startup CEO is a little crazy," says Matt Harada. "If they weren't crazy when they started the business, it is likely that the business will make them a little crazy. There are many paths that are so much easier. I don't think this excuses them for occasionally being incredibly hard to work with, but startup executive teams need to go in expecting this and learning to distinguish between working for a bad person and working for someone who is a good person who has bad days," says Harada.

ONBOARDING SUCCESSFULLY AS A STARTUP LEADER REQUIRES BALANCING SHORT-TERM WINS WITH LONG-TERM PRIORITIES

Executives need to understand which tasks to take care of right away and what processes need to be built to support long-term growth. Questions leaders should investigate in their first 90 days:

- What should your organization start doing, stop doing, and continue doing?
- Are there underperforming employees? If so, let them go as soon as possible.
- Who in your company is already an ally and who is "caustic" to your organization?

"I spent a lot of time in my first six months in an executive role making 'friends' with all the other executive team leads through 2x/month 1-on-1s," says marketing executive Matt Heinz. "It paid off. They like me now. They trust me now. Especially starting the role during pandemic remote-ville where they all already had physical-real relationships they established in the office prior to my arrival. Now I'm using all that capital I built up."

SETTING YOUR OBJECTIVES AND KEY RESULTS (OKRs)

Working with your CEO (or person to whom you report, if you roll up to someone else, like a COO or CRO), startup executives create OKRs that define success for their function and roll up to larger business goals.

While your startup may call them something else, the philosophy behind OKRs and goal setting on an annual, semi-annual, and/or quarterly basis is that they provide the north star to drive business growth, alignment, and accountability at the individual, team, and company levels. For your department and for the individuals on your team, OKRs provide a framework for measuring success. OKRs at startups are generally meant to be somewhat difficult, meaning they're orienting everyone towards goals aligned with significant startup growth. (Small returns aren't the name of the game.)

OKRs are the objectives and corresponding key results that startup teams and employees commit to each quarter to ensure alignment around business growth and maintain accountability at the company, team, and individual levels. When defining OKRs at the individual and team levels, you'll also tend to give them a weight reflecting the portion of time/effort you're going to allocate to this area. For example, if you're a sales leader, your primary objective will be directly tied to revenue.

This is true of sales as a team, and also for individuals at the team level. For every team and individual on your team, you'll have your primary OKR, as well as additional OKRs that contribute to overall success in your area. For your department and team, you'll identify the key objectives that roll up to the overall business goals and will focus the most effort on these areas.

According to Jack Altman, Lattice CEO, company goals should help employees to prioritize and focus, track progress, be motivated, define career development milestones, connect initiatives across a business, and give employees "direction while supporting their autonomy."[1]

Different startups measure success differently. Take whatever goal tracking system your founders and your executive team have decided upon and use it to build departmental and individual business goals.

For example, let's say a business goal is to get to $10 million in Annual Recurring Revenue (ARR) by the end of the year. Working backward, sales will develop objectives and key results that map to this business goal; they'll need to back this number through hiring reps, and building and closing pipelines. Marketing will need to generate a certain percentage of the pipeline (depending on the business model) for sales to hit their targets. Product teams may need to reach certain milestones for building features that the company can sell at a higher annual contract value (ACV) to hit the target.

Every department, including yours, will have goals that roll up to the overall business objectives for that quarter, half, or year, and every individual on your team will develop goals that relate to the department goals. What's so great about this system is that every blog post, product roadmap update, and sales meeting is easily traced back to the "why" for the business. It helps to have a north star and motivates your team and the business to row in the same direction.

SETTING OKRs—EXAMPLE: SAMPLE MARKETING OKRs

Sample Marketing OKRs for Q2

Business Area	Weight	OKR	KPI
Enterprise	75%	Opportunity Generation— Marketing Qualified Opportunities (MQOs)	**120 New MQOs for Enterprise Deals** * $7 million sales forecast value of marketing pipeline for Q2
Middle and Bottom of Funnel Ownership	15%	Increase Sales Accepted Leads (SAL)	**Increasing SALs by 20% (300)** by end of Q2 (within target accounts)
Team	10%	Recruit and onboard Team (FT + vendors)	**Team onboarded and producing** by end of Q2

After setting your OKRs, you can use red, yellow, and green color coding to track programs, giving teams a snapshot of their department's performance and progress against OKRs.

Upon joining, you should define the OKRs with your CEO or direct manager for the startup, and then build your own team's OKRs and get approval. Once these are approved, you'll build them with your team members (or eventual team members if you're starting as a team as one), usually within their first 30 days to establish and sign off with you on their OKRs.

OKRs AND BONUS COMPENSATION

Most executive comp packages have an incentive component. OKR-tied bonus compensation is generally remitted in accordance with performance and designed to incentivize individual performance that directly aligns with business growth. Usually, you'll receive these incentives as part of your onboarding and re-evaluate them quarterly, semi-annually, and/or annually, depending on how your startup operates. If your offer package includes bonus compensation, confirm with your CEO and/or manager what the specifics are around this at your startup, and also understand how your team will receive their incentive compensation.

DELIVERING YOUR FIRST QUARTERLY BUSINESS REVIEW (QBR)

At the end of your first 90 days on the job, once you've established OKRs and started building your program and executing against your initial "move the needle" goals, it's common practice to prepare a quarterly business review (QBR) presentation to the board and/or your startup leadership team. When I had to first create one of these in my first executive role, I wished someone had given me the following information. I hope this will help you understand how to summarize your first 90-day results to showcase your performance and position yourself for future success.

HERE'S A GUIDE FOR WHAT TO INCLUDE IN YOUR FIRST 90-DAY QBR PRESENTATION

- **Overview**—Provide an agenda and introduce what you're planning to discuss during the presentation.
- **Wins**—What were the highlights and "points on the board" you scored during your first 90 days? Be sure to include metrics, performance against OKRs (if relevant), and any data you can share to validate the wins you're discussing.
- **Challenges and solutions**—Share your perspectives on areas of your program needing improvement or investment and proposed solutions.
- **Learnings**—What did you learn in the first 90 days? What assumptions did you have coming in about the business that you proved or disproved? What "fresh insights" can you share with the businesses' shareholders that only you can provide?
- **Opportunities**—How can you apply what you've learned to make an impact in the next quarter and beyond?
- **Feedback**—Invite feedback on alignment and priorities for the next quarter and beyond from the board and leadership team.
- **Appendix**—Add additional slides here, like links to your strategies or plans, metrics dashboards, wiki pages, OKR details, organization structures, etc.

Before delivering your 90-day QBR, it's nice to provide a written summary as a pre-read, along with the deck (slides) to the stakeholders with whom you're speaking. The written summary should include the following, but with more detail.

In a written summary (in document form) that accompanies your first 90-day QBR, include a breakdown of what was accomplished not just at a high level (what I include in the "wins" slide) but also what was accomplished at 30 days, 60 days, and 90 days at each area of your program. Zooming in provides the context for the high-level reporting you're giving in your deck so that even before you present (and after), everyone has a detailed reference. It's especially helpful if, like me, you're especially comfortable writing in longform. Email this and the deck to stakeholders in advance, and you'll have done well to present your initial impact, as well as convey to stakeholders how you'll succeed beyond 90 days.

In the next chapter, we'll focus on how to build key relationships to be successful in your first 90 days.

CHAPTER SEVEN

Build Key Relationships: CEO, Board, Team

You've defined success, and now you've got to *really* understand how to manage these key relationships: between you and the business, your team, your fellow executives, you and your CEO, you and your board.

Building key relationships is an essential part of being successful in your role as a startup leader. They develop over time, and they require, like all relationships, effort and attention. Many leaders in their first roles think their primary focus is "the work," and I've made the mistake myself in underinvesting in key relationships.

The benefits compound when you put in the effort to learn the work styles and motivations of your colleagues, CEO, board, and team. When something goes south in the business (which it undoubtedly will eventually), having reference points and a wellspring of trust is extraordinarily useful. "Building relationships" can sound squishy, but it's anything but. Particularly if you're a member of an under-represented group, building relationships with people who are different from you (and potentially homogenous as a team themselves) can be daunting.

There's a real risk many under-represented leaders face in "being themselves at work." Kim Scott in her book *Just Work* shares that after publishing her book *Radical Candor*, she received feedback from women of color that being candid at work was riskier for them than straight white male peers, due to racial stereotypes and bias. Scott wrote her next book in order to address disparities.[1] You can still build work relationships that are functional, even if you don't feel as free to be "authentic." The pressure to have an authentic work relationship adds yet more stress to leaders from under-represented backgrounds.

Let's discuss the ones that you'll need to build, and some practical tips for how to build them.

BUILDING A RELATIONSHIP WITH YOUR CEO AND/OR CO-FOUNDER

Every startup joiner needs to build a strong relationship with the CEO and/or co-founder. Setting up a regular, predictable cadence of meetings where the two of you will spend time together is a great way to establish this. The typical parlance for this is one-on-one (or 1:1), and this meeting can happen on a variety of schedules. It can help to schedule them twice per week to start, at least for the first quarter, one at the top of the week, and one later in the week, with a once per month 1:1 that's just about you and your topics and growth. Expect to walk your CEO through an agenda that you create in advance, planning to spend at least as long as the meeting preparing for it and building an agenda.

HERE'S A SAMPLE CEO 1:1 AGENDA

Title of Meeting
- ex/Finance/CEO Review Agenda

Last Meeting Follow-up
- Talk about anything that carried over from the last meeting that you actioned and need to catch up on.

Metrics and OKR Review (10–15 min)
- Discuss performance against OKRs and goals; this should be the bulk.

Strategic (15–20 min)
- Any items that fall under strategy, less tactical and more high-level (here's where I want to spend my marketing program dollars to generate the inbound pipeline we need to hit our revenue targets, let's talk through it, or here's the organization chart change I'm thinking for Q4 and why I think it'll accelerate our growth, etc.).

Other updates

Risks
- Talk about things that could be a risk for your program or the business, like not meeting a hiring goal, or whether the new hires on your team are ramping quickly enough to hit your forecasted targets, or if you're having a hard time with something that's not going well. Talk openly about risks as well as your plans to resolve them. This is the #1 way to build trust with your CEO, and failure to do so is the #1 way to break it. Do not cover over the mud; it will seep through eventually and the best leaders know this.

Process
- Any new process changes; implemented new systems, links to project management board updates, or any tools and systems updates that your CEO should be made aware of.

People
- Hiring, firing, management, contractors . . . how's your team? What's noteworthy?

Feedback (5–10 min)
- Ask for feedback from your CEO in every one-on-one. This is fundamental. Don't skip it. You can also get feedback on any of "their list" of things they've been thinking about mentioning to you but maybe haven't throughout the week. It's a good practice because it gives them a dedicated time to ask you about things and makes it less likely you'll get that 2 a.m. "free to chat?" message. (Note: you can totally set a boundary and not talk to your CEO or anyone at 2 a.m., but you get the point.)

Notes and Action Items
- Including notes and action items is a great way to ensure anything discussed gets acted upon. If you talk about rolling out a new events program in Q2, write it down as an action item and your plan to follow up on it, which you'll discuss in your next sync.

There are other ways to set up 1:1s, and your CEO may have other preferences. The key is for you two to meet regularly, establishing a cadence that enables you to report on the high-level performance of your team, share any risks or problems early, update on team items, and, crucially, get and give feedback. This is one of the most rewarding aspects of being a startup leader, so learn to love them! And if you can, in that once per month 1:1, come prepared with questions (lots of good ones out there) and areas to discuss that matter to you, like career growth, business vision topics, and more.

BUILDING TRUST WITH YOUR CEO: VALUES ALIGNMENT

According to Broadly CEO Mindy Lauck, trust around values is crucial for the working relationship between a CEO and executives.

"Everything hinges on trust," says Lauck. "You don't get trust in the first week on the job, trust has to build up over time. It starts with values alignment—values alignment, extremely open communication, and vulnerability with each other are the three ingredients that build up trust between a CEO and executive or executives with each other over time," says Lauck.

SET UP COMMUNICATION EXPECTATIONS WITH YOUR CEO AND LEADERSHIP TEAM

In the "always-on" world, it can be helpful to document your preferred work style, hours, and needs in a company wiki or shared document. You can also set up things like "async" chat channels in Slack or Teams where your CEO and leadership team can message you things that they don't expect a rapid response to (and vice versa). Be sure to also inquire as to what works best for your colleagues (and you can do this as you build your team, too). Startup leaders need to learn what their CEO prefers, rather than relying on just what they're used to.

GET TO KNOW YOUR CROSS-FUNCTIONAL PARTNERS AND BUILD RAPPORT

You should spend a significant amount of time upon joining and getting to know your cross-functional partners. Set up meetings and find out what they care about. Invest early in building trust with your peers in startup leadership including what their agendas are, and how you can help them be successful.

LEARN HOW YOUR KEY STAKEHOLDERS LIKE TO WORK

Find out what makes them tick at work. What systems do they prefer? What working hours do they like to keep? Do they prefer last-minute deadlines or do they tend to get things done ahead of time? Do they prefer written narratives, slides, or spreadsheets? Would they prefer to review things with you on calls with the agenda in advance, or would they rather you send everything to them and they can review asynchronously? Everyone works differently and learning the preferred styles of your colleagues, CEO, and board will help you adapt and succeed. And they can also learn how you work, too.

DON'T BE AFRAID TO DISAGREE—RESPECTFULLY

You don't have to be a "yes person" when you start working cross-functionally with peers. In fact, that's not helpful. I remember working with a sales leader who agreed with everything I did and said as a marketing leader, often only commenting with "great" or "looks good." While my ego enjoyed that at the beginning (really? Everything I do is coming up roses with sales?), I soon realized that our revenue organization truly needed a cross-functional partner who could respectfully go toe-to-toe with marketing and provide critical feedback.

If you have contradictory data or another way of looking at an issue, find the right time to make that heard. Constructive feedback is the lifeblood of start-ups, and if you build a relationship in a respectful way, you'll be able to give and receive feedback to help everyone around you make the best decisions for the company.

WHY COMPANIES BRING IN "BIG COMPANY EXECUTIVES" AND HOW TO WORK WITH THEM IF YOU'RE COMING FROM A STARTUP BACKGROUND

The "march of the incoming senior executives" happens frequently around a fundraising round. Startups bring on seasoned leaders who can theoretically come in over the managers who have helped the startup get to the stage where it is, then scale each business area leveraging their experience. This is often at the behest of their board, who want to be sure that the startup brings in people who can be trusted to deliver (because they've proven to have done so in the past). Sometimes, that even includes a new CEO.

If you're working with "big company" executives as a startup executive who's come up through those ranks, here's advice for navigating those relationships:

- **Learn what you can from the big company executives and don't discount their experience.** They may know how to navigate the byzantine procurement process with your customers. They may know how to build a team of 40 people when you've only managed a handful of folks. They may have wonderful advice about how to invest your 401k. Take their experience seriously.
- **Be willing to teach them new tricks, if they're open to it.** Many big company executives coming into the startup environment know they may be out of touch with the tactical. If you have that experience, and they're open to it, you can offer tremendous value to them.
- **Be patient if big company executives act a bit formal.** Many big companies encourage divisions and politics and that's not personal to you. If you feel

that a big company executive talks down to you, you may be right, but it's probably unintentional. Try to find ways to get to know them as people, what matters to them, and be patient as they're learning to operate in startup environments.

BUILDING STRONG RELATIONSHIPS WITH YOUR BOARD

Depending on the maturity of the startup, you may meet your board prior to joining as part of the vetting process in evaluating you for the role. Alternatively, you may be aboard for a year or more without ever interacting with the board, connecting directly with your founder. Often, boards have programs that are meant to "add value" to their portfolios. They may have content programs or provide presentations that you can consume. Investors often run series for helping go-to-market teams by bringing the best and brightest among their portfolio companies to teach others in the portfolio a key area of expertise. Attend these kinds of events if you can.

MANAGING TO YOUR BOARD'S EXPECTATIONS

As you work with the board, you'll be focused on optimizing for contributing to business growth, understanding market trends, and working with them to build the best business possible. They can pattern match across many businesses and see markets in a different way than many of us who are operating tactically. And they may need your help to see how the tactical and strategic work you're doing relates to the bigger picture of growth. Learning to think "at the board's altitude" will serve you well as you grow in your startup leadership career.

LEARN THE INTERESTS, HOBBIES, AND FAMILY MEMBERS OF YOUR EXECUTIVE TEAM

Especially now that many of us are working remotely, it can be hard to get a true sense of our colleagues. We miss out on body language, desk photos, seeing how they behave in the physical world. Take extra steps to do small talk and get to know your team, including their interests, hobbies, and family members.

I keep a notes document on my phone listing the names and ages of my colleagues' kids and pets, as well as the names of their partners. (Note: I found all of this out by asking them, not by doing invasive sleuthing. I don't trust my memory for these details, so if I want to retain them, I have to write them down. People genuinely want to share most of the time, and, of course, if they don't, be respectful of their boundaries.) I make a note of colleagues' birthdays and their favorite hobbies. If a colleague likes to surf, I will ask them about surfing and do some research to understand. This may sound like a lot of "non-work" work, but remember how good it feels when someone learns something specific about you? To build rapport, share common ground, and learn what matters to your colleagues.

CHAPTER EIGHT

Know Thyself: Strengths, Weaknesses, and Areas to Improve

> *As you set up for success, you need to take stock of your weaknesses, especially those resulting from never having done this job before. It's okay, everyone has them. The key is to strategically knock them out.*

You have strengths and unique talents that you'll bring to your role as a startup leader. You also, like all humans, have areas that are *not* strengths, aka weaknesses. Some of these weaknesses can be improved upon, and you'll benefit from investing in growth, while others, you will need to strategically work (and hire) around. We'll cover how to determine the difference between the things to improve and the things you'll accept and work around. The good news is that you don't have to be perfect and have every aspect of the startup world or even your function down before going for an executive role.

Often, people from under-represented backgrounds can hold themselves back from reaching for their goals because of the belief that you have to have *all* the strengths humanly possible and no weaknesses. This perfectionist belief can hold you back from recognizing your own unique gifts and capabilities as a startup leader.

Let's talk about how to recognize your strengths, areas that are not currently strengths, and learn to improve in key areas that count while working around areas you don't want to improve.

YOUR RELATIONSHIP WITH YOURSELF AS A STARTUP LEADER

Your relationship with yourself is the bedrock of any relationship you'll build at your company. By better understanding your own needs, background, sensitivities, strengths, and weaknesses, you'll have more freedom in navigating others' differences.

You've known yourself your entire life. You've known losses and triumphs, and you've hopefully gained self-awareness from your experiences along the way.

(Note: Jerry Colonna's book *Reboot*, David Richo's book *How To Be An Adult*, and Tara Brach's book *Radical Compassion* are great places to start if you're thinking of exploring additional self-inquiry tools.)

While you've been physically present for your own experience, most startup leaders reach a new level of success only when they take time to truly become aware of and develop compassion for their own experience in the world. What triggers you to feel defensive, or angry? What contexts make you feel competent and what areas do you naturally excel in? What makes you feel unappreciated or what situations make you feel afraid or angry? What kinds of activities make you feel a sense of what researcher Mihaly Csikszentmihalyi calls "flow," when you're fully immersed in what you're doing and a sense of magical ease permeates throughout?

Being an LGBTQ+ woman forced me to confront many aspects of my experience in the world and self-reflect at an early age. My identities have given me a path to explore that led to unveiling around my own privilege, and how that was affecting my relationships at work and beyond. We all carry multiple identities. By understanding and having compassion for your own experience, you'll bring more compassion for others and theirs.

IDENTIFYING YOUR STRENGTHS

Often, our strengths are so second-nature to us that we don't even recognize them or properly value them. Tools like StrengthsFinder are a great option for understanding more about what you're uniquely good at and can bring to an organization. Strengths you may already have that position you well for your leadership role might include:

- Deep expertise in a functional area after years of experience in, for example, finance, operations, marketing, sales, etc. You know your tech stack, your tools, and what counts in your area.
- You know the customers and industry that you're hoping to lead in. Bonus points if you have personally faced that pain point. For example, I worked

at a two-sided B2B SaaS marketplace startup in the construction technology space, and those of us with construction backgrounds had an easier time understanding the ideal customer profile than those of us who just had a background in B2B SaaS, or in marketplaces.

- Experience with the startup stage and growth stage you serve. Most founders, according to Elad Gil in *High Growth Handbook*, want executives who can do the job for the next 12–18 months[1] rather than looking for people who have already proven they can scale to the stage of growth 5 years out. So if you've done the startup stage where you're hoping to lead, that's helpful. (It's an easier pitch to say hey, I've helped companies grow from $1M to $5M ARR vs. someone with that experience trying to lead at a $50M ARR startup.)
- Project management skills. You may know how to project manage for success and work well with partners and other cross-functional teams, even if you've never held the "head of" title before.
- Excellent written and oral communication skills. Many great writers take it for granted. If you can document, present, and otherwise "share the knowledge" internally and externally, that's a big boon to your startup.
- Collaboration skills. The ability to collaborate and work well with others is a crucial skill for startup executives.
- Amazing depth in one particular part of your field. For example, you might have deep subject matter expertise in outbound or account-based marketing. While as the functional leader you'll own more than this, don't discount the areas that are your strengths already. For instance, I spent more than a decade in customer-centric content marketing and community and brand marketing prior to owning a marketing team and all areas of a marketing organization, which became a superpower as I scaled. I did, however, have to learn more about adjacent parts of marketing that I hadn't led before, like Product Marketing and Demand Gen.
- Excellent quantitative and analytical skills and learn how to manipulate data and tell a compelling story around your analysis.
- Ability to galvanize a team and motivate people towards achieving a goal. This is an underrated skill in leaders, and if you've got it, don't discount it as "soft"!

Self-assessment is a lucrative industry. From hiring executive coaches, to 360 reviews, Enneagram, DISC, StrengthsFinder, and other assessments, there's no shortage of opportunities to invest in understanding yourself and your team. I don't have a strong opinion about the best growth tools. The ones you find to be helpful are probably a good bet. As a startup leader, you want to get feedback and data to learn from, and you need to find ways to filter and action that feedback.

Questions that can help us identify strengths:

- What expertise have I developed in my field thus far? *Am I a skilled coder and can bring that technical expertise to my role as a technical leader? Do I have a deep background in demand generation that as VP or CMO I'll bring to the table?*
- What leadership skills have I already developed? *Can I write and communicate clearly and effectively? Do I have management experience (even if it's just contractors)? Am I comfortable giving talks and doing public speaking?*
- What do I do that I take for granted that others praise me for? *According to Erin Rand, things people compliment us on and we take for granted are often secret superpowers.*

WEAKNESSES: THINGS THAT MAKE YOU FEEL IMPOSTER SYNDROME UNTIL YOU ADDRESS THEM

As a mid-level manager or even director, your remit is often one specific area. You have weaknesses, but you can just work around them. It's easier to lean on one area of strengths in earlier roles because your role is narrower.

Executives lead an entire function, which will eventually include areas in which we're not as experienced. We don't need to know how to execute everything, but we need enough insight into the purpose and goals of the function to successfully understand the "why" behind what that area needs to perform. For example, startup executive Matt Harada didn't know how to be a controller prior to his first Head of Ops role, but he knew what a controller needed to do for his Ops team and was able to hire the right, experienced person to fulfill the role's remit. Addressing these weaknesses will require some coaching and learning.

EXPECT TO HIRE AROUND YOUR WEEKNESSES BUT SEEK TO UNDERSTAND THEM AND NOT AVOID THEM

I have a background in content, customer success, community, and communications on the marketing side. Marketing operations is not my primary strength. Because I know this, have recognized it, and have made peace (to some extent) with the fact that I need to hire people with strengths in these areas within my program to balance what I bring to the table.

The natural tendency among leaders is to hide weaknesses or pretend they don't exist until they make up for them. This is a huge waste of time and can reinforce imposter syndrome among executives. This is particularly true for those of us from under-represented minorities where if we don't know something, it's not naturally assumed that we are the right people for the job and if we don't know something, we can work around it.

The automatic assumption might just be, "They're not executive material," and that's not right. Rather than hide my gaps, I am upfront about them in new roles. With any weakness, try to understand it, get curious about it, offer yourself some compassion (we all have weaknesses), and decide what you're going to do about it so it doesn't thwart your success on your executive path.

UNDERSTANDING HOW TO HANDLE WEAKNESSES

If you're reading this book, you probably want to improve some areas of your startup leadership. So how will you identify what you'll work on, and what you'll hire around, or leave to other superstars on your team?

MEASURING YOUR EFFECTIVENESS AS AN ENGINEERING LEADER: GET HONEST ABOUT YOUR SKILLS AS YOU TRY TO LEVEL UP

Engineering leader Jeff Ammons helps aspiring engineering leaders he mentors grow through implementing a metrics-driven scale to take the guesswork out of advancement.

Ammons advocates using a ten-point scale for technology, people, process, and product.

"I would say people need to be at least a six in all of those categories in order to be a functional manager, and then ideally I would want them to be better, say at least an eight, in one category as a starting manager," says Ammons. "I want to make sure that they've demonstrated competency at a six out of ten in all those other areas before I take a leap on them," says Ammons.

Ammons says that by measuring skills, his leaders can see how to improve based on merit.

Ammons says this is in stark contrast to any idea that an engineering leader "just needs five years" or some other arbitrary amount of time in order to get the experience, because some people can develop the skills quicker, and some never do.

"Asking for feedback is a great way to improve. You're going to progress much faster due to compounding returns on your skills. In other words, do you have ten years of experience or do you have one year of experience repeated ten times?" says Ammons.

BEING HONEST ABOUT OUR STORTCOMINGS: ENTREPRENEUR RAND FISHKIN'S PERSPECTIVE

Startup entrepreneur and author Rand Fishkin has built successful companies and is involved with efforts to help make startups more inclusive for everyone. He's noticed a pattern of "hiding" flaws at many companies, which is something I've seen too. It can be human not to want to be seen as not good enough or not equipped to succeed.

"In ninety-five percent of organizations, people cannot be honest about what they're not good at, because you are not rewarded for honesty and transparency about your mistakes and inexperience. And this is true ten times over if you are a woman and/or a person of color or anyone not perfectly checking the box of straight-cis-white-male," says Fishkin.

"Because I am in my 40s, straight, stylish, white, male, people have given me a lot of room for error. They say, 'you know, if he says he doesn't understand something, we'll give him a pass.' For people who don't look like me, that's near impossible. The incentives just aren't there," says Fishkin.

"Surviving in a corporate environment often means to lie and misdirect or to sort of lie through omission," says Fishkin. "The culture can be to then go figure it out on our own time, learning those practices nights and weekends and upgrade our skills or hire people on our team who are great at it."

"If you can, leave those jobs where you can't be honest about your weaknesses and be a part of companies where you can build psychological safety and a great culture," says Fishkin.

IDENTIFY: WHAT ARE YOU NOT STRONG AT THAT YOU'LL WANT TO IMPROVE?

These things can include:

- Subject matter expertise. What parts of your department do you lack expertise in? What doesn't come naturally to you, whether that's a part of your function that's highly qualitative or quantitative, or requires technical know-how that you (at least currently) lack?
- Knowledge: product, knowledge about your company or market, the latest insights about your department or area (for example, what are the latest sales tools or revenue recognition best practices?).
- Delivery: learning how to make effective slides. Are you weaker at organization and/or writing? Will you need to hire someone who can help you become better at delivery?
- Executive presence: public speaking, how to build frameworks, create business theories.
- Subject matter expertise in your department, tool knowledge, increasing confidence, etc., are all things you can work on with a coach.

HIRING FOR COMPLEMENTARY SKILLS

As leaders, we need to hire people who have skills and experience that complement our own. If we needed all of the experience and skills ourselves, we'd wait a lifetime to be leaders. Are we more "creative and big picture" and not as detail-oriented? We can hire people who can excel in areas we don't.

GOING DEEPER: GETTING TO KNOW OUR MOTIVATIONS

Everyone is motivated by different things; your startup leadership journey may be motivated by wanting to learn, increased financial gain, a sense of fulfillment, or to create healthier patterns on teams than you experienced, and/or all of the above. Learn and become comfortable with your own motivations to know better how to work with them.

Coach and author Jerry Colonna says, "whole, better humans, make better leaders, requiring radical self-inquiry to unpack our patterns."

FOCUSING ON ADDING VALUE, REGARDLESS OF TITLE

Startup leader Sarah Innocenzi has held numerous executive-level startup roles throughout her career, including VP of People and Chief of Staff. But ultimately, she realized, adding value regardless of her role or title was most important to her. She surprised even herself by realizing she wanted to prioritize her impact over her title.

"Most of my early career was about climbing that ladder and getting myself into these more senior roles. When I reached my goals, I realized that I still wasn't fulfilled," says Innocenzi.

Innocenzi decided to explore a larger organization where she could be supported as a leader but not necessarily at the executive level. When she decided to bring her startup executive expertise to a larger organization, she knew she'd be leading, but with a different title.

"I've really started to rethink the idea of exploring slightly larger businesses where I would have experienced mentors that can add value to me and my career development," says Innocenzi. "But there's definitely a scary ego check that has to happen when making a transition away from the executive-level I have worked so hard to achieve."

EMBRACE IMPROV AS A WAY TO BECOME A MORE PRESENT, COLLABORATIVE LEADER

Startup executive Colleen Blake often prescribes improv to her leaders on her team. When we worked together, I started improv classes at her behest, and I found it to be fun and invaluable for teaching me public speaking skills that come in handy in many leadership settings.

"Improv teaches you how to be a better listener," says executive Colleen Blake. "When you're brainstorming on a strategy, being present and really listening to what the other person is saying opens up many possibilities."

GET TO KNOW YOURSELF THROUGH "PERSONAL RETROSPECTIVES"

April Wensel, Founder and CEO of Compassionate Coding, an organization that helps companies create more compassionate workplaces and technology, suggests that all startup leaders conduct a "personal retrospective" to get clear on what really matters to them at work and in their careers. Here's April's advice for the personal retrospective.

Exercise: Personal Retrospective, by April Wensel

- Time allotment: minimum 5–10 minutes
- Materials: paper and writing utensil or computer

Sit quietly and reflect on the following prompts, and then write down your responses:

- What do you really care about in life? Give 3–5 things.
- What are your personal values?
- What are places where you're living according to your personal values, and where are you not?
- What do you need to change?
- What specific steps can you take toward making those changes?
- Plan another retrospective for next month to check in on your progress and adjust your action plan as needed.

"A lot of times we get stuck in autopilot," says Wensel. "People get locked in positions where they're not happy. If you're unhappy and struggling, it might be time to leave that job."

Wensel says it's okay if we don't take all of the steps we've identified right away. For example, some people may not feel comfortable quitting right away.

"If that's the case, you can still start to make an escape plan. Living fiercely according to your values requires taking risks, sometimes going against the grain in order to stand up for what you believe in," says Wensel.

Similarly, Asana CMO Dave King suggests doing a "happiness and fulfillment timeline": King recommends an exercise that he learned at the Stanford Graduate School of Business while he was an MBA student. King says he "bifurcates happiness and fulfillment because people often mistake the two."

King says after the birth of his first daughter, his wife was sick and in the hospital for three months. He was caring for his newborn and managing his startup leadership job at the same time.

"It was not a happy time of life, but it was super fulfilling," says King. "I look back and I go, that was an experience that brought us together."

What times in your life were you happiest and most fulfilled that you can draw from as inspiration as you chart your next course?

Exercise: Happiness and Fulfillment Timeline by Dave King (Adapted from Stanford Graduate School of Business)

- Time allotment: minimum 5–10 minutes
- Materials: paper and writing utensil or computer drawing software

Draw the following:

- Draw a line chart of your life, starting at age five, as early as you can remember to the present day.
- On the *y* axis, write happiness and fulfillment.
- Draw a line chart where for over years of life, where are those peak moments of happiness and where there were low moments of happiness and fulfillment.
- Think about how topics like family, exercise, profession, and community factored into your happiness and fulfillment.
- Chart those things over life and look at where passes and troughs are and what was going on, and what does that say about me and what I value.

King and his partner do a quarterly "offsite" where they get away for a day, have a nice dinner, and carve out time to see if they're living according to the values they've outlined as a couple.

"You go through seasons where you're out of balance, and you recognize it and want to get back in balance," says King. For example, his partner recently moved from Google to Lyft, and the new job, new team, new working hours, and more travel threw the family dynamics a little out of whack. When they identified this as a couple, they decided King was going to spend a little more time at home to accommodate his wife's new schedule. "We knew that at a certain time we'd get our stride again," said King.

King emphasized that for those who do this exercise, there's no right or wrong answer. It's based on the things you value. King said he and his family value things like urban amenities, being able to walk to school, and rarely using a car.

"In San Francisco, I have a short commute after dropping the kids off at school," said King. "Other people will take an hour on the train, and they value that train time to work and decompress. For me, that would not lead to good mental health. I'd rather be at work or with my family. Even a little bit of exercise or biking is restorative and energy-producing. A commute for me would be energy-draining. We may sacrifice to live in the city. If we lived elsewhere we could have more of a yard or various benefits."

UNDERSTANDING OUR PRIVILEGE AND HOW IT IMPACTS OUR WORK

No matter your background, we *all* have work to do to understand privilege and how it operates in our workplaces and the world.

According to psychologist Melanie Joy PhD in *The Vegan Matrix*, "a privilege is an advantage, practical or psychological, that one person or group has and that is denied to others."[2]

Joy says "privilege exists only in relation to others . . . privilege is a key element that keeps systems of oppression alive. It's often invisible, and without realizing it, our privilege causes us to defend, rather than challenge, oppression."[3]

Our privilege can impact how we lead in big ways. By doing work to understand how privilege operates in our greater society and within our companies, we can take the steps necessary to question our beliefs and feelings and see how, as Joy calls it, "privilege has taken over our psyche."

For example, as a cisgender LGBTQ+-identified woman, I need to understand Joy's concept of "privilege literacy" around genderism because transgender people are likely to be negatively impacted if I am *not* aware of the ways genderism functions and my potential role in reinforcing problematic stereotypes and discriminatory genderism behaviors. Because of the way power and privilege function, Joy suggests, in this example, those without cisgender privilege are less likely to be blind to its effects.

According to *The Memo*, author Minda Harts shares in her chapter "No More Passes: For My White Readers":

"You might be shocked at the experiences women of color face in the workplace and how some white people have played a role in making it harder to ascend. As a first step, I need your mindset to change; no longer can you run to your safe space and assume we aren't moving forward in our careers because we aren't working hard enough or aren't qualified, or that we experience the same workplace inequalities because we are both 'women' . . . for real change to happen, you must listen and be open to unlearning what's been comfortable."[4]

It is the responsibility of everyone at a startup to work on not acting out their biases and causing harm to those around us. This work is not just the responsibility of one group and certainly cannot rest solely on the shoulders of those who come from under-represented backgrounds.

Author and technologist Susanne Tedrick shares in her book *Women of Color in Tech*:

"Solutions to problems this systemic cannot be made in isolation and require hard work and conversations by everyone."[5]

EMBRACING ALL OF OURSELVES, INCLUDING OUR "SHADOW" SIDES

According to coach and author Jerry Colonna, the "shadow" is Jung's place where we put "disowned partners of ourselves. For many of us, we may have grown up learning to disown parts of ourselves in order to be safe," says Colonna. "If we grew up socialized to be 'men' we may not have had much tolerance or room for our feelings. If we grew up learning that being outspoken would label us 'aggressive' and a 'problem' due to our race and/or gender, we may have learned to hide those parts and be overly people-pleasing and quiet, which can hurt us in leadership roles where we're required to take action and make decisions and speak confidently about our opinions."

ARE YOU OUTSOURCING A PART OF YOURSELF TO YOUR TEAM?

As adults, our work as leaders may be to recognize and own our shadow parts to ensure we're not acting them out in strange ways.

Colonna shares a story in his book (and shared with me on a Techstars mentor call) that he once coached a CEO who had hired "a greedy person" whose greed frustrated him.

"The breakthrough moment for him was when I said, well, who hired this guy?" says Colonna. When the CEO replied, "Well, I did?" Colonna reminded him that he knew this about this leader when he hired him.

Upon reflection, this CEO admitted that he had grown up very poor, addicted to alcohol, and had run away from home as a teenager and was homeless. He deeply wanted to have "enough" which his unconscious had labeled "greed" and buried.

"He outsourced his sense of greed he did not accept within himself," said Colonna.

Colonna said that those of us who have power are "especially susceptible to outsourcing the disowned parts of ourselves to parts of the organization. We break the pattern of distorting the organization when we take ownership of the parts of ourselves," says Colonna.

CREATING HEALTHY BOUNDARIES

It takes time to truly understand yourself and what boundaries you need to be productive at work and in life, but the process pays dividends.

According to startup marketing leader Allen Chong, healthy boundaries improve his job satisfaction—and performance. "My team noticed I was happier and more productive when I stopped taking work with me in my off time," said Chong.

"Learning how to create our own boundaries is key," says Google events and experiences manager Alana Corbett. "No one will do it for you. Having internal self-awareness of when I'm starting to feel burnout, I know I need to create a day off Friday. I can work more in the sprint and rest periods vs. feeling it's never-ending."

Corbett runs experiences that can draw thousands of people. She relies on rejuvenation after busy events.

"Knowing your limitations enables you to really stretch and be safe," says Corbett.

CHAPTER NINE

Learn the Company Culture and Define It with Your Team

How does your company work, especially in the remote-first post-Covid world? What's the wiki? How do you collaborate? What are company norms and cultures? As an executive, you're setting the tone for your team, and you're also working within a broader organization. Here's how to get in deep so you can set yourself up to win.

A startup's decisions are driven by its values. These values impact everything from how vendors are treated to how much budget is allocated to employees' desks to parental leave and more. According to a recent Deloitte Millennial Survey, millennials want to work with mission-driven companies that align with their values.[1]

UNDERSTANDING STARTUP VALUES

Each startup operates within an implicit or explicit value system—a set of principles that guides every aspect of the startup. Values help companies orient and make decisions when they reach impasses.

The company's values provide an answer to the question: "Does this align with what we want to achieve?" and should be consulted before proceeding with any major decision.

COMPANY VALUES DRIVE BEHAVIOR

Whether implicit or explicit, these values impact behavior. For instance, at an early-stage startup I worked for, even before the value was written explicitly (it was later codified in the company wiki), we all knew that we were supposed to treat contractors and vendors with as much respect as our customers and employees.

The CEO made it clear that when in doubt, we would err on the side of generosity in our contractual agreements and that every vendor left us better than they found us. (Unfortunately, many startups and larger scale-ups *do not* treat contractors and vendors with this respect or value them appropriately.)

OTHER WAYS CULTURE IS IMPACTED BY VALUES

Values encompass major company policies, like recruitment, offboarding (aka letting an employee go), employee benefits, remote work setups, and even how the company responds to competitors and government bodies. See Uber's history for context on how their original values shaped their behavior towards the competition and government. Changing their values with the help of fresh leadership in the form of Harvard Business School professor and co-author of *Unleashed*, Frances Frei and new CEO Dara Khosrowshahi massively impacted the successful refurbishing of their public image.

Company values shape every experience you will have at a startup. Here are a few examples of stated company values:

- Share The Knowledge (ServiceRocket)
- Don't #@!% the customer (Atlassian)
- Judgment (Netflix)
- Courageous Hearts (Headspace)
- Always Grow (Ping Identity)

CREATING A HIGH-PERFORMANCE, SUPPORTIVE CULTURE ON YOUR TEAM

It's up to you as a startup leader to form and cultivate an outstanding team and to build a strong and supportive company culture where people exceed goals while also feeling supported to do their best work. The culture you build will be an extension of the company's values but will be unique to you and your team in its expression.

There is not just one culture within a startup; as Venture Capitalist Brad Feld calls it, this is because everyone hired creates a "culture add" (as opposed to "culture fit," which can perpetuate bias in hiring).

BUILDING TRUST AMONG YOUR TEAM AS A STARTUP LEADER

As managers of teams, startup leaders must guide and support people and build trust and belonging. These days, more employees are vocal about wanting high-performing work cultures that also feel supportive on multiple levels.

133

Author and executive coach Kaley Klemp advocates for a mindset of radical generosity in leadership, particularly around including everyone's boundaries in agreements.

"Priorities are what you say 'yes' to. Boundaries are what you say 'no' to. You need to have a conversation in teams about your shared guidelines. Ask: 'What are our agreements? What do we say, 'Yes' to? What do we say, 'No' to? When do we revisit a decision around a yes or a no?" Klemp says these questions are key aspects of "Conscious" leadership on teams. (Read her book *The 80/80 Marriage*, co-authored with her husband Nate Klemp, for more about priorities and boundaries, and *The 15 Commitments of Conscious Leadership: A New Paradigm For Sustainable Success*, co-authored with Jim Dethmer and Diana Chapman, for more on these topics.)

CREATING A CULTURE THAT ISN'T "ALWAYS-ON"

A healthy team environment requires healthy boundaries and expectations around how work gets done. Set defined work hours and respect people's lives outside of work. Be clear with your team what your expectations are around how often people communicate and give people ways to set healthy work boundaries.

CREATING INCLUSIVE TEAMS WHERE INDIVIDUALS FROM DIVERSE BACKGROUNDS CAN EXCEL TOGETHER

At scale, many larger companies have increased attention to diversity and inclusion (D&I) efforts, allocating budget to D&I roles and building these efforts into the employee experience. Unfortunately, this is less common in earlier-stage startups. If you're joining an early-stage startup as an under-represented leader, you'll be getting extra attention. As an openly LGBTQ+ woman tech executive, I'm always humbled when a team member tells me in private that they felt comfortable joining because I'm a member of the leadership team. Never underestimate the value of visibility in creating inclusive teams.

Some great books devoted to learning how to build inclusive teams include:

- *Unleashed: The Unapologetic Leader's Guide To Empowering Everyone Around You* by Franceses Frei and Anne Morriss
- *Women of Color In Tech: A Blueprint for Inspiring and Mentoring the Next Generation of Technology Innovators* by Susanne Tedrick
- *The Memo* by Minda Harts
- *It's About Damn Time: How to Turn Being Underestimated into Your Greatest Advantage* by Arlan Hamilton
- *Mental Health And Wellbeing In The Workplace: A Practical Guide For Employers And Employees* by Gill Hasson and Donna Butler
- *How To Be An Inclusive Leader: Your Role In Creating Cultures Of Belonging Where Everyone Can Thrive* by Jennifer Brown

Inclusion is about fostering a non-homogeneous work environment that promotes and retains based on qualifications, not external characteristics, such as:

- Ethnic and racial diversity
- LGBTQIA awareness
- Cross-cultural awareness
- Accessibilities
- Disabilities
- Age and ageism
- Religion

CREATING "BALANCE" ON TEAMS

People leader Aubrey Blanche advocates creating "balanced" teams, and argues that many companies focus on the wrong metric when it comes to diversity and inclusion on their teams. Blanche says that individual team inclusion metrics are significant; focusing on aggregate data, Blanche argues, can mislead statistics.[2]

Balance, Blanche says, is about team leaders as much as company D&I or HR professionals, so take it upon yourself to learn how to build repair and take responsibility for creating an inclusive environment.

CREATING HEALTHY WORK EXPECTATIONS THAT SUPPORT INCLUSIVITY AMONG YOUR TEAM

I once worked for an executive who liked to work late. As a working parent, she frequently got her best work done while burning the midnight (and later) oil. I'd frequently see late timestamps on her work or project management system updates. But she always made it perfectly clear that she did not expect her team to work late, despite her preference and schedule. Sometimes, I decided to work late, but I never felt pressured to do so. I suspect it was the same for our team.

A healthy culture allows for a manager to work in their best way, and their team to work in theirs. Some leaders will snooze notifications after certain hours and/or encourage their teams to do so. They will forbid weekend emails. Using tools to support boundaries is great, but it could be even simpler than this. Just set clear expectations about the boundaries you expect for your team.

That's what teams are for; we cover for each other. We can creatively work around each other's schedules while honoring the work that needs to get done. We honor each other's health and wellbeing above work products because we know a strong work product results from us feeling strong and being strong as whole human beings.

CULTIVATE PSYCHOLOGICAL SAFETY ON YOUR TEAMS

According to Gill Hasson and Donna Butler in *Mental Health And Wellbeing In The Workplace*, "People need to feel psychologically safe . . . In a team with high psychological safety, each person feels safe to take risks and be vulnerable around others. They feel comfortable expressing themselves and feel safe that no one will undermine them, embarrass or punish anyone else for bringing up problems and tough issues, for speaking out about concerns, making and/or admitting a mistake, asking a question, asking for help, or offering a new idea."[3]

Psychological safety on teams benefits *everyone*. For your direct reports, for their families and friends, your decision does the hard work of cultivating compassion and being respectful. Even if (especially if!) you have to fire someone, you can do it in a respectful way that is honoring them as an individual (even if it is still a hard conversation).

COMPASSIONATE BOSSES MAKE PEOPLE'S LIVES BETTER, SO ASPIRE TO BE ONE OF THEM

"The more you get into leadership, the more opportunities you have to do harm due to your blind spots. Don't project your stuff onto your team," says D&I expert Aubrey Blanche.

Ways you can be a compassionate boss and contribute to a culture of psychological safety include:

- **Processing your own emotions, including anxiety and anger, *before* reacting.** This includes not impulsively sending heated communications to your team, but rather sitting with your strong emotions and *then* communicating.

- **Understand your biases and practice respect for people's individuality.** Be aware of your own biases and work hard to check them so that you don't inadvertently discriminate or create a hostile work environment. Everyone has biases. We all have to learn how to recognize them and not perpetuate discriminatory behavior.
- **When you make a mistake or misstep in a situation with a team member, own it and make a plan to improve**. Don't expect others to make you feel better about your mistake. For example, if you make a comment that offends someone based on identity, commit to improving and don't make the issue about the other person.
- **Encourage your team to seek appropriate support.** If something happens that violates an employee's rights or boundaries, do not dismiss their concerns. Encourage team members to get help from HR or People Ops and be willing to help them seek those resources. In this vein, leaders often go into "hero" mode and try to solve all problems. You have limits, and you are not their therapist. Accepting this is both annoying for people who love to think they have ultimate control, and also highly freeing because it lets you be a part of the solution while knowing you're not the only (or best) resource to resolve issues in most cases.
- **Understand that your team's health and wellness comes above work, always.** Don't expect your team to put their wellbeing ahead of the company's needs. Be aware that people will go through periods where they need more time off or flexibility. As long as they're accomplishing their goals, do not fault them or cause them to feel guilty and pressure them to put their own wellbeing on hold for the company's sake.
- **Be compassionate towards yourself.** Do your own inner work with a coach, spiritual advisor, or therapist to understand your needs and communication style better so you can learn better how to work with others' needs and styles.

Emotional maturity and compassionate leadership make a difference in people's lives. You don't need to be a healthcare worker or a teacher to have a positive impact on people's wellbeing and personal development.

GET TO KNOW YOUR TEAM AS INDIVIDUALS

Part of relationship-building is getting to know the strengths, preferences, and weaknesses of your team. For instance, my leadership team values my empathy, to the degree that when I get a "spidey sense" about a candidate, my team pays extra attention. Sometimes even I don't value it as much as my team does. That's a smart way of making the best use of the "pool" of skills.

Esther Perel says at work, "people show up with two resumes: their CV and their relationship history."[4]

What Perel is alluding to is that we all have different "baggage" so to speak from past jobs or even relationships. We see our work and our world through the lens of past experiences and help people on their journeys to be themselves and do their best work.

PART III

BUILDING AND MANAGING YOUR TEAM AND DEPARTMENT

CHAPTER TEN

Recruit Smart and Build Belonging

> *Your people matter, people. Here's how to build a superlative team, with some pitfalls to avoid.*

W hether you've inherited a team or are building one from scratch, as a startup leader, you'll need to learn how to successfully lead a group of individual contributors and managers.

RECRUITING NEW TEAM MEMBERS

While you'll ideally have a People Ops/HR recruiting team at your startup, your success depends on your ability to recruit people with the skills and experience to deliver outcomes for your team.

Anyone you hire must align with three areas:

- The skills and experience required to meet the business objectives of the role in your organization (that tie into the company's larger business objectives).
- The company's values and cultures.
- Your team's unique culture.

That's a lot to balance, right? There's a reason why hiring is one of the most valued startup skills. It's one of the biggest jobs of a team lead.

Many executives, unfortunately, churn because of their inability to hire and retain top talent. Hiring talent who will scale is hard. It sounds obvious, but if you can't build a team effectively, startup leadership is impossible. You need to convince talented people to join your company, but more than that, to join *you* as a boss.

This is even more true at smaller startups; larger companies or scaleups benefit from their size, and if someone doesn't like working for one manager, they may switch teams or departments (even within the same organization). When you start having skip levels (people who report to your direct reports), people may quit *those* people, which is why hiring great managers is so essential.

WHAT TO DO IF YOU'VE INHERITED A TEAM

Just as you may inherit legacy software or tools, you may also inherit a team. Often, team members at an early-stage startup will be generalists, and you'll need to staff up with specialists to be successful.

Often you're brought in because they've had only generalists with little experience in your functional area in the past, so you'll need to do an assessment and perhaps shuffle the players. As they grow, startups bring on more specialists, so building your team may include letting go of early-stage generalists or finding them a new home, either on another team or outside of the business. Don't immediately discount the generalists on your team; you may benefit from the institutional knowledge they've acquired.

Upon inheriting a team, these are things to assess:

- What skills and value (including historical knowledge) do team members bring?
- What gaps can you hire to fill?
- Are there underperforming team members who aren't in the right role fit and who may need to be transitioned to another team or out of the organization?
- Historical insights into how this team was working before you joined; what worked, what didn't?

HIRING YOUR TEAM

You'll want to work with your CEO to map out your organization chart and identify how to align your people with the goals you've set out to achieve. Often, hiring coincides with funding and growth milestones. You'll need to forecast headcount and justify why you're spending in key areas.

DESIGNING YOUR ORGANIZATION CHART

As you join your team, you'll be expected to understand and build out your organization chart. At early-stage startups, many of the initial hires will be generalists. You'll need to come prepared with past hires from the former teams you can pull from (honoring any contractual agreements, of course) and/or a plan for your organization.

Building your organization chart at a very early-stage startup may be as simple as writing your name and circling it. As you grow, you'll need to scale the team and key players. A great way to de-risk hires at very early-stage startups is to hire agencies or consultants to prove the value of the resource. For example, a hiring plan for a growing early-stage marketing team might look like this:

Q1—FTE: You (VP of Marketing) + Consultants and Agencies (SEM/SEO, brand, product marketing, content, demand gen and ABM, automation, PR, BDR)

Q3—FTE: You + Demand Gen and ABM Senior Manager, BDR, Head of Product Marketing, Head of Content, and agencies (SEM/SEO, brand, content writers, product marketing, PR, content, demand gen and ABM, automation)

Q4—You + Demand Gen and ABM Senior Manager, BDR, Head of Product Marketing, Head of Content, Content Marketing Manager, and agencies (SEM/SEO, brand, content writers, product marketing, PR, content, demand gen and ABM, automation)

Etc.

HIRING TIP: CREATE A SCORECARD

Partner with your HR/People Ops team to create a scorecard with candidate skills and experience. This ensures that you're honing in on exactly the right attributes your hires will need. Rank the skills in terms of how important they are in the role (0–4 scale is fine) and weigh each area in percentages adding up to 100%. For example, x% of the role requires Recruitment and x% is managing our applicant tracking system or ATS, etc. With a hiring scorecard, interviewers will not accidentally evaluate candidates differently based on their own ideas of what should matter. If someone has a lower score on something that's less crucial to the job, take it into account as a "would be nice" vs. "must-have."

Scorecards equip recruiters to target the right talent and disqualify candidates without the key skills. They also prevent them from disqualifying potentially great talent because of a misunderstanding of essential job qualifications (another source of bias in the hiring process). They help everyone to assess candidates and identify the most qualified folks.

REDUCING BIAS IN THE HIRING PROCESS

Look for culture "add," not a culture fit, as venture capitalist Brad Feld says. Be clear about what's required of the job, in contrast to what's simply nice to have. (This is also a way to reduce bias in hiring.) Instead of trying to preserve the "culture" of your team, understand that every new person adds different skills and characteristics. Aim to see each new individual for their own merits, recognizing that their unique needs and attributes will diversify your team—and that's a good thing.

Note: "They seem like the kind of person I'd like to have a beer with" is not an acceptable "culture" hiring criterion! (Feel free to grab a beer with whomever you'd like, but don't hire someone because they seem like a good drinking friend. That's just going to reinforce stereotypes.)

CULTIVATING EQUITABLE, DIVERSE, AND INCLUSIVE TEAMS

According to a McKinsey study[1] from May 2020, diverse companies are more likely to hire and retain the best quality talent and perform better in competitive markets. Depending on your organization's maturity, you may have explicit D&I initiatives in place, but it's every startup leader's responsibility to contribute to and create a safe and welcoming environment that supports and includes diverse talent.

There are entire books dedicated to eliminating bias in hiring and creating diverse teams. For the purposes of this book, understand that startup teams have a lot of power to shape the industry. As your company champions increasing inclusion, work with your hiring team to help them understand the kinds of questions they should be asking employees and how to reduce bias in the hiring process. Make sure that under-represented individuals on your team (including you, if that's the case) aren't discriminated against when it comes to promotions and salary, or excluded based on identity.

HIRING PEOPLE: HOW TO RETAIN TALENT ON YOUR TEAM IN TODAY'S COMPETITIVE LABOR MARKET

In *The Alliance*, authors Reid Hoffman, Ben Casnocha, and Chris Yeh outline a framework for thinking about the relationship between employees and their employers. They refer to "tours of duty," specific missions that employees sign to understand that in our at-will labor market, both the company and the employee need to provide each other with value.[2] The types of tours can be "rotational," which they describe as being short term for entry-level employees, usually one to three years; transformational, or determined by a specific mission, usually two to five years; and foundational, which is ongoing, for those employees who align with the DNA of the company.

Employees are engaging in transactions with employers. While previous generations may have stayed at the same job for their entire careers, in today's labor market, startup employees can quit a team and company at any point, and they can be asked to go in most states at any point "at will." If you hire people with a mutual understanding of your expectations for them and the value you'll add to their lives and career goals, and if the other elements of the equation align (compensation, benefits, interest in the work, etc.), you're in a great place. If you understand that at some point that will end, and it doesn't have to end in fire and brimstone (for either side), it sets a healthy, realistic expectation that work is mutually valuable and fulfilling while not necessarily forever.

CHAPTER ELEVEN

Alignment: Set the Strategy to Get Your Team Working Toward the Same Vision and Goals

> *Get the strategy right and don't micromanage. An executive needs to scale her-self, and here's how to do it by setting the vision.*

D elegation is the transfer of true ownership of a task or set of tasks to someone else. On startup teams, we're all moving fast, and microman-agement breaks at scale.

As a startup leader, your role is to show your team the vision, so they can adopt it and create value. As you develop your leadership style, there are many frameworks to choose from. But as organizational psychologist and executive coach Dennis Adsit suggests, "having a framework—*any* framework—to test and see if it fits, is infinitely better than just doing 'jump ball.' "

HELP YOUR TEAM TO UNDERSTAND THE MISSION AND THE "WHY" BEHIND THE STRATEGY

To set the goals for your organization, you first need to know the mission you're on. For instance, if you're a SaaS sales leader, your mission is to increase revenue by growing the customer base and/or increasing customer lifetime value (LTV). Note that your mission doesn't have to be exclusive to your team; the marketing team at a SaaS company is also focused on driving revenue and the customer success team is focused on expanding customer lifetime value through delivering success. If you're a marketing leader, your mission might be to drive awareness and build thought leadership, while also increasing revenue and growing the customer base, etc.

When you set a mission for your team, it helps both your own team and other organizations to know if you're following your organization's charter and they can weigh that against every decision. (Will this increase awareness of our business and/or grow revenue? If not, let's reconsider.) There may be times your organization strays away from your core mission, and if this happens enough, it's worth re-evaluating whether it makes sense to expand or change your mission. For example, you may add to a sales team's charter to "expand existing customers and increase their customer lifetime value alongside customer success."

SETTING OKRS WITH YOUR TEAM

As you've set your organizational OKRs, you'll need to set OKRs with each individual on your team to enable them to succeed and grow in their roles. Their OKRs should roll up to your department goals, which roll up to the overall business goals.

BONUSES TIED TO OKRS

If your team has a bonus compensation structure, clearly define what measurements contribute to bonuses and how employees can achieve them. Your company may outline a bonus compensation structure and document a company-wide policy eventually (they should), but often it's on you as a manager at an early-stage startup to confirm and coordinate those details.

Compensation is sacred. Startups often leave bonuses in a gray area, causing stress for employees. If you set an expectation that an employee will receive a certain bonus if they achieve certain outcomes and don't deliver, or even deliver it late or in a way other than communicated (e.g., if you promised quarterly but then move it to annually), it will damage your relationship with your team. Prevent misalignments down the road by communicating upfront the specific, key results that must be achieved for attainment, what dollar amounts those will correspond to, and how and when those will be remitted.

UNDERPERFORMING TEAM MEMBERS

When It's a Temporary Thing

Sometimes startup team members underperform for a short period of time. This is often due to overwhelming or external circumstances that won't have a lasting impact on their ability to perform work. They may miss a deadline or fail to hit a goal. In your 1:1 check-ins, it's important to understand whether their performance is due to something that's happening in their worlds and/or if it's a temporary issue. Don't leap to the conclusion that all is lost if they're having an off day or week or month. We all do sometimes. Ask questions to find out what's at play and be empathetic to them while also figuring out solutions together for ensuring key work tasks in their area are accomplished.

When the Performance Issue Doesn't Improve Over Time

Some startups have what's called performance improvement plans (PIPs). Managing people out of the business by first documenting the performance issues through a formal plan is a typical strategy for transitioning out underperforming team members. Most startups in the US, however, have at-will employment, and so it often doesn't come to a PIP.

If you're at the point of putting someone on a PIP, usually you already know what you want to do and are documenting it for legal purposes and to give the employee notice. Sometimes people can overcome the PIP and improve, but it's not likely. That's why it's important that before any official or unofficial PIP, and/or before managing someone out, you should communicate clearly that they are not meeting standards. Telling someone "you're not meeting my expectations in these ways" may sound harsh, but it's the kinder choice than what Kim Scott calls "ruinous empathy" by which someone continues blind to their lack of performance and doesn't have a chance to either course-correct or transition of their own volition.

GET IN THE WEEDS IN ORDER TO UNDERSTAND THE NATURE OF PROBLEMS

If you don't pay close attention and spend ample time understanding the ins and outs of your team's work, you can miss key issues. This doesn't mean constantly micromanaging. Once your team has something under control, and you're confident in how a process or team area is working, you can zoom out. But if something *isn't* performing, or it's a new function, strategy, or tool, you need to understand it. You can't rely on another's word for it, even if you truly do give them ownership. Spend time in the weeds after delegating by understanding what your reports are doing on a microlevel, even if you're not the one doing it (or dictating it). Observing and asking questions are the key methods to finding areas that need attention. You may discover your assumptions don't hold once you hold a magnifying lens to an issue or program.

LEAD WITH THE BEHAVIOR YOU WANT TO SEE

As all parents understand, regardless of what you say, people will observe and react to your behavior as much as to what you say. If you tell your team to always come to meetings with agendas and prepare, but you don't do the same, they'll notice and are less likely to take you seriously. If you speak disrespectfully to team members, even the ones to whom you've never spoken in this way will notice. If you don't use your project management system to track issues or work, your team will see that and be less likely to think it matters that they log all of their work. This isn't to say you have to act perfectly, all the time. Teams are generally forgiving when you own up to mistakes or inconsistencies, but strive to have your behavior match what you want to see from others.

CONFLICTS ON YOUR TEAM: HOW TO IDENTIFY AND WORK THROUGH THEM

Katrin Grunwald, coach at The Globe Team, says conflicts are natural, but we need to deal with them effectively as early as possible. She suggests leaders ask themselves, whenever a conflict arises on their teams, "who should be involved with regards to solving the conflict?"

Solve conflicts at the appropriate level. A conflict that isn't loaded is easier to solve than one that hits at people's identity.

"Once you're at the identity level, that's when things get really tough and that's where as a leader for you it's important to see who's involved," says Grunwald.

PAY ATTENTION TO THE DETAILS LONGER THAN FEELS NECESSARY

According to author, entrepreneur, and executive coach Kim Scott, author of *Radical Candor* and *Just Work*, "we can't fix problems we refuse to notice."[1] Workplace injustices are intersectional and, as leaders, sometimes we may inadvertently cause harm. "Only when I recognize the way my privilege harms others can I lay it down."[2]

Peter Drucker famously said "management is doing things right. Leadership is doing the right things." Empowering yourself and your team to "do the right things," regardless of your rank, is crucial. Executives at startups do this by building a clear strategy tied to goals, which enables every team and person within your team to know the right things to work on and create value.

CHAPTER TWELVE

Attunement: Creating a Culture Where People Contribute Their Best Work

> *Leadership isn't born; it's taught. It's surprising how many startup leaders lack training in this area. Get these fundamentals down and watch your team perform far above their punching weight.*

Attunement is a concept in psychology that stems from a core human need to be seen, recognized, and honored as individuals. This happens with startup founders naturally; think about all of the founder-specific decisions companies make. Here are a few ways I've seen attunement play out for founders at companies:

- A poker-themed company holiday party because the founder famously loved to gamble.
- Violin giveaway at a high-tech conference when our product and brand had nothing to do with violins or music because the founder was a violinist.
- Very few meetings, because the founder disliked them.
- Lots of meetings, because the founder liked them.
- No alcohol served at company parties, as an unwritten rule, because the founder didn't drink.
- Lots of IPAs always served at company parties, as an unwritten rule, because the founder preferred them.
- The office was located in a city that was easily accessible by the founder to get to his kids' school from his home, even though no other employees lived in that very expensive area that was a long commute for most of the team. When the idea of moving to another city closer to the majority of the staff came up, it was shot down, primarily because it would have been inconvenient for the founder.

Some of these become so baked into company culture you'd have to really trace it back to uncover it's about one or two people's preferences. These preferences become like the laws of physics at tech companies. Attunement is possible at the individual level, from the co-founders to the lowest-level startup employees. Enabling others' contributions rather than delivering your own requires understanding of how to empower the individuals on your team as individuals. This is also the best way to support a diverse group—expending energy to truly understand and meet diverse needs. In this chapter, we'll tackle strategies and tips for success.

BEGIN WITH THE GOAL IN MIND: EMPLOYEE EMPOWERMENT

Most startups regularly set goals with objectives and key results, defined by measurable results (OKRs, etc., as discussed earlier in the book). To reach company goals, you'll need to reach team goals, and those are achieved through individuals meeting *their* goals. The unit of collaboration means empowering your startup team to deliver. Getting everyone rowing in the right direction and working on the right work is hard. It takes a lot of systems and intention to disrupt a new market. To guide your cadre of joiners to accomplish goals requires that they understand and take ownership of their areas and contribute.

Think about the best boss you ever had, and how this person treated you. It is likely they:

- Helped you always understand the team vision and strategy, even (especially) during times of ambiguity for the business.
- Helped you clearly understand your OKRs and/or individual goals and how those rolled up to the team and overall business objectives and mission.
- Encouraged you and believed in your ability to grow and accomplish more in your job and career.
- Trusted you to accomplish your work and let you truly take ownership vs. micromanaging every aspect of your work.
- Gave you a sense that they cared about you as a human being and not just for the work product you produced.
- Made it safe for you to make mistakes as long as you learned from them and to prevent making the same mistakes in the future.
- Were kinder than they needed to be.
- Treated you as an individual and didn't unilaterally impose their style and preferences on to you without understanding how you work best and what your styles were.

As you work to become a better startup leader, think of becoming the kind of boss who makes people feel seen, more supported, challenged, engaged, and encouraged. The growth that's possible professionally when we have a supportive leader is simply astounding. The more work you put into becoming a supportive leader, the bigger the impact you'll have not only on business outcomes but on people's lives.

MAKE BUILDING A HEALTHY CULTURE A TEAM PRIORITY

The choice to build a healthy team starts with you. Prioritize creating an environment where people can thrive.

"As a manager, I know that I need to have an impact not only on business outcomes but on people's lives. When I bring that awareness to my team, the drive to make the project a success improves tenfold," says engineering leader Stephon Striplin.

Building healthy processes and resources, you'll empower your reports to deliver more value and be happier at work.

TEAM EMPOWERMENT STARTS WITH BUILDING TRUST

Anne Morriss and her co-author Frances Frei say that the best teams include "high standards, authenticity, and empathy."[1] Whether you inherit a team or build one as you join, invest in building trust with your reports as soon as possible. Understand that everyone's individual work styles, as well as their personal preferences around work communication and style, will need to factor into how you lead them. There is no "one size fits all" approach to management, but rather a constant calibration against the individuals whom you're managing.

Your team will also be getting to know you and your work style and, together, you'll all learn how to work as a group (fun, right?). In your management, relate to your team members as individuals with their own style, meaning your style will need to adapt somewhat to each report. An extrovert may want to interact differently from an introvert, etc. Diverse and inclusive teams require accounting for everyone having different needs and styles.

GET SUPPORT ALONG YOUR JOURNEY THROUGH A SUPPORT CIRCLE

Kalev Kaarna, VC at Superangel in Tallinn, Estonia, says that for his startup portfolio, he always recommends—and even pays for—six months of leadership and personal growth coaching for its leaders specifically so they'll build healthier companies. He says in addition to this, he also supports creating "mastermind" groups for the functional area executives. "You don't need permission to do this," he said. "Anyone in the startup community can create a group of five or six people to meet and be each other's support."

A coach or "support circle" can be a great place to vent to neutral parties so you're not offloading your angst to your reports. Managing (and tending to) your strong negative emotions and refraining from projecting them onto others is your number one priority as a team leader. In my opinion, this action alone is the single most powerful thing you can do in the tech world to make people's lives better.

ENSURE YOUR TEAM HAS ENOUGH RESOURCES TO BE SUCCESSFUL

Having enough resources improves the lives of those on your team. Preventing burnout on your team isn't just about giving people advice on how to set boundaries and practice self-care on a personal level. Adding more responsibilities to your team in a cash-strapped startup is tempting, but you need to resist unrealistic expectations. Often, high-performing individuals will meet them at a cost to themselves. Even if you don't care about someone's happiness (you should!), that person will be more likely to quit, meaning you'll lose your valuable resource.

To fuel sustainable growth, a startup must bring on more resources, including full-time employees (FTEs) and agencies and consultants in any area where your team is overloaded, and in new growth areas.

It's one thing to ask team members to take on stretch projects for their own career growth while helping them de-prioritize other areas. It's quite another to ask your head of content to now build a new user community and monitor it several hours per day while also QA testing the app. As you mature in your role, anticipating where you'll need more resources and investing in them early (before it becomes a painful situation) will save you and your team headaches.

LET YOUR TEAM KNOW YOU, TO THE DEGREE YOU FEEL COMFORTABLE WITH

As an openly LGBTQ+ woman in tech, I've been surprised by how many of my team members and members of other teams have confided in me that they are LGBTQ+ or have a LGBTQ+ family member. I think it puts them at ease to know that they are not alone and to see representation. Being open yourself can make it feel safer for others on the team.

I know a lot of executives who are working parents who are honest with their teams about their struggles (and joys), and who have said that this is crucial for creating the authenticity culture on their team.

As a team leader, you'll have to decide what makes sense for you. Not everyone feels comfortable or has the same privilege to share parts of their identity, particularly depending on where in the world they are working and the type of startup. Don't feel you have to over-share or put yourself in an uncomfortable position. The idea is to reveal and open up parts of yourself that will help people see you as an individual, which in turn can give them more permission and freedom to be their own individual selves. That authenticity can go a long way to build trust and create a safe environment in which to solve the tough problems startups face.

EMPOWERING YOUR TEAM TO DELIVER AND LET GO OF TASKS IN YOUR "ZONE OF EXCELLENCE"

Executive coach and venture capitalist Sue Heilbronner says leaders that she coaches were often promoted based on the skills that they exhibited as individual contributors.

"In the early phases, it gets very difficult to let go of performing those individual contributor tasks in your 'Zone of Excellence,'" says Heilbronner, referencing Gay Hendricks' concept of "Zone of Excellence" vs. "Zone of Genius," which refers to working in areas that we are truly genius at versus just excellent at. For example, think of a world-famous artist painting vs. driving a car. They may be an excellent driver, but it is not necessarily their "genius."

Heilbronner and Hendricks describe the "zone of excellence" as things that you're really great at but they're actually not the things that are going to carry you into the highest level of success in an executive role.

"Because those things are so comfortable and because you've been praised your whole career for doing those things, it's difficult to let them go, not as a delegation issue, but as just a habitual issue, you're used to doing them as one person," says Heilbronner.

BUILD PSYCHOLOGICAL SAFETY BY CREATING AN ENVIRONMENT WHERE MISTAKES ARE HANDLED WITH CARE, NOT BLAME

Startups require learning; you're testing assumptions and getting data from the market. Sometimes, these tests don't work out. If we make a place for learning and growth, we're able to move faster than if we create an environment where mistakes are hidden due to fear of retribution.

When we openly learn from our own mistakes, we also engender a sense among our team members that they, too, can make mistakes, and make amends for them. This flexibility creates a healthier team dynamic than one that purports not to ever make mistakes (impossible) and acts from a place of perfectionism. In the repair process with our teams—the coming apart and coming together again—we can learn how to build healthier workplaces, as well as healthier environments for people to thrive as individuals.

Teams make mistakes. Retrospectives are at the heart of agile methodology for a reason—they enable us to learn, adapt, and grow faster. Startups themselves are a metaphor for trial and error, an attempt to boldly disrupt an industry, in the vulnerable state of not knowing for sure how things will turn out. Unlike established enterprises, vulnerability is baked into the heart of startup life.

That's not to say that you shouldn't address continued mistakes; if an individual or if your team is continuing to make the same mistake, that needs to be discussed and dealt with. No matter what, however, you can treat the mistake harshly while treating the person or people involved with kindness and respect. Getting this right is one of the best things you can do as a boss. It's worth investing time to work on learning how to treat yourself with kindness when you also make mistakes.

CONSIDER INSTITUTING A "NO MEETING" DAY

When it comes to managing health and wellbeing at work, taking a day per week focusing on doing deep work and taking breaks from endless meetings can help your team deliver their best. Many companies are now doing this; consider it for your organization.

A WORD ON BEING A MEMBER OF AN UNDER-REPRESENTED GROUP AND NAVIGATING MAKING MISTAKES

Based on conversations with friends who are also leaders from under-represented backgrounds in the startup world, there can be more pressure on us to not make mistakes or to do everything "twice as well" because we are sometimes not assumed to be qualified or to be fit for the role based on industry biases.

With such low percentages of people of color, LGBTQ+ people, and women of all backgrounds in startup leadership, we can feel added pressure to "get it right" all the time. That kind of pressure is exhausting and unfair, and, frankly, is unrealistic, because all startups require making choices, getting data on whether they succeed or fail, and then learning from them.

Recognizing the issue is the first step in creating space for change, so notice and pay attention to situations where you're putting extra pressure on yourself and/or your team to perform "perfectly" and see if it's possible to still continue to perform without chasing the unattainable "perfection" goal. It can help to get feedback from peers and mentors, particularly others from under-represented groups. Get positive feedback on your accomplishments as well as get support in this area of perfectionism due to imposter syndrome or fear of failing if not delivering perfectly all the time.

CREATE A ROADMAP WITH INDIVIDUAL PREFERENCES AND AGREEMENTS FOR WORKING TOGETHER AS A TEAM

Consider creating a "how you work" strategic document, including preferred communication channels, schedules around everyone's time zones, preferred ways of working, and more. You can keep this in a company wiki or a shared doc with your team. When you're clear about your own boundaries and needs, and encourage your own team to do the same, it is easier to work together.

Think of these as "unauthorized guides" to working with you. Include everything from your operating approach, how you like to do 1:1's, manager handbooks, and the ins and outs of how you think about working. You can also include how you approach chat, what your work style is, what you expect of your team, and what things don't work well for you. These things all help those who work with you (your own team members and other teams) to learn quickly how to meet your style and adapt to your needs. What a time-saver. Consider doing one of these for your teams so they can know you better sooner, and you can reduce friction working together.

CHAPTER THIRTEEN

Building a High-performance Team Culture

Learn how to inspire and coach your team to achieve when you're not around.

Every team is made up of individuals with different needs, abilities, and styles. The "culture" on your team can and should change over time as your team grows. Leadership experts and authors Anne Morriss and Frances Frei say that both "presence" and "absence" leadership are crucial elements of management. This means that the leadership impact you have extends beyond moments where you're actively involved, or even in the room.

You are responsible for building a psychologically safe work environment that enables your team to achieve your collective goals. This includes helping your team learn how to operate independently and as a group.

"We are imperfect humans leading imperfect humans, by definition," says Morriss. "We are going to build imperfect companies."

You and others on your team will make mistakes, and the key is to practice repair and learn how to adapt and come back stronger than before.

STEPS TO BUILDING A CULTURE OF SUCCESS

In order to build a culture of success in your team, you'll start with building relationships, as you did with your managers, as well as creating a rhythm around helping your team goals.

CREATING A PERFORMANCE CADENCE WITH YOUR TEAM

Daily
- **Daily virtual and/or async standups** (depending on the organization)

Weekly
- **Weekly 1:1**
- **Weekly team meeting**, which is less of a status update, more where each member of your team can share Wins/Highlights, Challenges, Upcoming Team changes/PTO, and Asks for Help, and you check in around department OKRs. They should fill this out in advance in a Notion or Wiki doc and/or shared slides.

Biweekly/Monthly
- **At least biweekly or monthly "Career" 1:1** that's just about individual team members' career goals, personal topics, anything they want to chat with you about.

Quarterly
- Discuss direct reports' OKRs for the upcoming quarter as well as review their wins, challenges, and learnings from the previous quarter.

THE 1:1S WITH YOUR DIRECT REPORTS

Your reports should create 1:1 agendas shared in an ongoing, updated doc in your wiki or docs that follows similar formats to your CEO 1:1. They should highlight what's going on in their department, discuss their progress against OKRs, and get your feedback. They should also have space to bring up concerns or issues before they become larger.

CREATE BETTER 1:1S BY ASKING BETTER QUESTIONS

Great managers ask their direct reports great questions. Asking better, open-ended questions is crucial to a successful one-on-one or any meeting between you and your reports.

Questions like:

- What does success look like?
- What are the obstacles?
- What are the options and next steps?
- What are your thoughts on this so far?

As the department lead, your job is to help your direct reports clarify their thinking, to understand the work they and their department are doing toward department goals and company goals, and to help them get unstuck.

GOAL SETTING AND OKRs

Create a rhythm around individual OKRs that roll up to group OKRs, as you do for your team and its department. Make sure your reports understand the prioritization and weight of goals. For instance, driving pipeline revenue and opportunities may be weighted as the most important goal, while a goal around implementing tools and processes contributes less to their overall goals and bonus compensation.

Communicate with your reports what you expect them to deliver, what success looks like, and what a big win would be. A note: goal setting should be aspirational. If you set goals that are too unrealistic or too easy, neither sets your team up for success. Set goals that push your team to deliver their best work, while rewarding truly outstanding outcomes. If your startup is open to not capping bonuses (it depends on your department and various other stages), giving your reports the chance to earn even more than 100% of their bonus can be highly motivating.

CARVE OUT TIME TO TALK CAREERS AND GIVE FEEDBACK

Schedule a 1:1 for each of your direct reports to talk about their goals and their career aspirations. You may make assumptions about what your reports care about that they don't share. It truly depends on them. For instance, I once asked one of my marketing reports what his vision was for his career, and he told me bluntly that he wanted his current role to be "his last W2" and be in business for himself after accomplishing his mission in his current role. I never would have known that, and if I'd assumed he'd wanted to become a CMO one day, I'd have managed him incorrectly. Never assume. Ask your reports regularly what their goals are and look for ways to help them meet those goals.

SMALL GESTURES ADD UP TO A CARING MANAGEMENT STYLE

Kindness and caring are under-rated in leadership. If you pay attention to your reports, truly listen to them (stop multi-tasking during your 1:1s!) and give them the gift of your undivided attention when you can, it'll profoundly impact their ability to be successful on your team. Listen to what they care about and ask them how they want to grow.

If a report of yours wants to learn a specific skill set outside their role, you could look into giving them stretch assignments or helping them tap into company learning and development resources to take a course. Sometimes, small gestures like letting the report know you believe in them in what they hope to accomplish can make the world of difference. Don't underestimate the power of believing in people on your team. You can be that person that helps your reports build their own journeys and you should let them lead the way while offering new ideas if they're open to them.

MEETINGS: HOW MANY DO YOU REALLY NEED TO BE IN?

Often, early-stage startup leaders will be in too many meetings with their team and cross-functional peers. While meetings are a crucial part of your role, at a point, you need to delegate and have your leaders take them on your behalf. You can always attend strategically or once every few meetings, but you can't be in every meeting all day. If you go through your calendar and find it filling up with many meetings (particularly cross-functional ones without your peers), see if you can take yourself out and review the notes. This is great for many reasons, in that it truly empowers your reports and frees you up to do more strategic work.

IS THIS MEETING SET UP TO FAIL? HERE ARE WARNING SIGNS THIS WON'T BE A PRODUCTIVE MEETING

- No agenda.
- You're in attendance but neither contributing nor adding value.
- People aren't prepared prior if there are things to review together (particularly cross-functional meetings; no one wants to wait while someone tries frantically to create reports on the fly).
- Misalignment between meeting goals and meeting actual. (Is it a meeting designed to get clarity on a topic and people are debating another topic? Focusing on what the meeting is supposed to do is helpful.)
- No clear action items after. (All meetings need some agenda items after so it's clear what's next and who is accountable. For instance, in a cross-functional meeting between sales and marketing after a field marketing event, it should be clear what marketing will do to follow up with the attendees and no-shows and how sales will follow up with their named accounts, etc.)

MANAGEMENT TIP: DON'T SEND "CAN WE TALK" MESSAGES TO YOUR TEAM

If you don't give context, a majority of the population will suffer a jolt of anxiety when receiving a vague message out of nowhere from their manager that simply asks "to talk." No matter how secure a relationship is, this is scary to the human nervous system. Imagine receiving this from your CEO, or from your partner, or a random friend . . . particularly out of the blue. See? Nerve-wracking. Our human brains are wired to detect threats in this sudden unknown.

Don't send ambiguous messages to your boss either if you can help it; it works both ways. In the absence of context, humans often assume the worst. Especially in our remote world, even a bit of context can put people at ease. If you have to schedule a last-minute meeting, try to give context so your report doesn't assume the sky is falling.

BE EMPATHETIC TO WHAT PEOPLE ARE GOING THROUGH WHILE SETTING HEALTHY BOUNDARIES

Everyone going through the pandemic faced unprecedented stresses—some more than others. You never know what someone is going through. If someone slips on performance or an assignment or doesn't communicate, or a typical extrovert is unusually quiet, it could be something in their personal life that's throwing them off and don't jump to conclusions.

You also don't need to be your reports' therapist; it's a balance, but understand when you're feeling depleted and out of your depth. It's okay to say "I'm not the right person to help you through this, but I want to encourage you to get support with the resources our company offers and/or outside of work."

You can set boundaries around where you can support. It's totally fine to listen and part of being a manager means finding out about people's personal lives (that's not a bad thing). Even if you *are* a licensed therapist, that's not your role as a startup leader; leave that to professionals to give people the advice, support, and care they need (and deserve).

Some things you can do other than provide "therapy:"

- **What kind of support do you need?** Do they need help in accessing the company's benefit policies around mental health and/or support in the area they're needing? Maybe they just want people to give them space. Others may want to process (and it's okay if you set a boundary around helping them find other outlets for that support.).

- **Do you need to take some time off in accordance with our time off policy?** Sometimes people are just burnt out and it can help when managers point them to take their PTO and not let it lapse. You'd be surprised how much can be solved by time to "unplug."
- **How can our team support you better?** Sometimes people could use extra support at work around a project or campaign, say if they have a sick family member or something is going on that's distracting them for a short time. While in the long term this would need to be addressed, that's what teamwork is about: supporting each other and helping each other around difficult times and celebrating the wins together.

BUILD FEEDBACK INTO YOUR REGULAR COMMUNICATION AND PROCESSES

In *Radical Candor*, Kim Scott famously shares the danger of "ruinous empathy," or being so empathetic and concerned about people's feelings that you fail to give them the honest, compassionate feedback they need to thrive. Often people can miss the feedback that something is awry unless it's given early and often. Make it a habit to carve out time in your 1:1's and team meetings to review progress against goals and share areas to work on. Also, be open to feedback from your direct reports to improve. It'll feel awkward, but it's worth it.

Retrospectives are a great tool for teams. Questions to explore in regular feedback:

- What is going well?
- What is not going well?
- What could we be doing differently?

- What are we going to start doing?
- What are we going to stop doing?
- What should we keep doing based on what we've just learned?

Pauses to truly reflect and learn make the difference.

BEWARE THE PITFALLS OF "SKIP LEVELS"

Katrin Grunwald, coach at The Globe Team, suggests being careful around "skip levels," aka interactions with your managers' team members, and ensuring that you're not going around a manager to speak with their team members either. "Assuming good intent, you're disempowering your leaders if you're not letting them do the work of managing their own team," says Grunwald.

It's great to schedule a regular biweekly or monthly 1:1 with your skip levels, and many organizations advocate for this to gain a better understanding of their worlds. It's also a chance to assess how your reports are performing and how their reports are doing. If you do need something from one of your direct report's reports, work with your direct report. The same rules apply if you need something from one of your peer's reports. While this is a startup environment and we're all collaborative, honor the reporting structures put in place at your organization in order to work most effectively and efficiently.

SOLVING CONFLICTS ON YOUR TEAM

Conflicts can fall into various categories. At the highest level, they're about work itself (tasks, etc.), then roles, behavior, values, personality profile, identity. Conflicts at the bottom (identity) are tricky. You may think you're talking about changing the air conditioning, but let's say you've read the study that women tend to prefer and need warmer office temperatures than men. For a woman on your team, your insistence on keeping the office cold becomes an identity and belonging issue. The point is, conflicts can happen at all levels, and resolve them by understanding the level.

ENSURING YOUR TEAM (INCLUDING YOU) TAKES ADEQUATE TIME OFF

Many startups these days offer "unlimited PTO." This can be a benefit for many reasons, and also can trap people into feeling guilty about taking time off. While it's great that companies are starting to set "suggested minimums," in reality, if you as a manager don't encourage and model taking time off, your team will struggle to do this. You want your team to take time off and rest; it's good for them, it's good for the overall team. The global pandemic blurred boundaries between the personal and professional, and made it even more crucial for people to invest in time off.

TAKE TIME TO REALLY UNPLUG YOURSELF TO SHOW YOUR TEAM THAT'S THE CULTURE

When you take off, it makes your team relax when they take off. It can be hard in our always-on economy when there's never really a time that's truly convenient to be out of pocket, but you have to do it. Take time off from work, and you'll return better for it. Managers, team leaders, and individuals have to take responsibility for their own health and the health of their team. It's not just because it's good for you as an individual. It's truly the best thing for the output of the team.

Move It!

In the book *Tech Stress*, author Dr. Erik Peper says stress requires some discharge of the energy that's built up. "The best way to get rid of mental stress and strain is to work it off physically," says Peper.[1] If you're thinking about starting

174

health-affirming individual practices, *Burnout* by Emily and Amelia Nagoski is another great book to help guide your journey.

CULTIVATE AS FLEXIBLE A WORK ENVIRONMENT AS POSSIBLE

Studies from LinkedIn show that as offices are opening up, many under-represented folks are in a worse position than when they were able to work remotely during the pandemic (while dealing with a lot of other trauma and issues, of course). The reason for this is that many modern offices did not create healthy nor supportive environments for everyone. Women of color, in particular, found more discrimination and challenge in office environments that did not cater to their needs.[2]

From struggling to meet discriminatory dress codes to needing to "code switch," under-represented folks can struggle in homogeneous, open office work environments. Parents, people caring for family members, and other groups need flexibility around work hours and how work gets done.

Office environments can be *very* tricky for people of all backgrounds, particularly for those who studies show benefit from flexible work and flexible work environments. It's not just the commute people dislike. It's what happens in these physical spaces that can prioritize certain people's boundaries and needs over others, and cause some to have to "code switch" and turn off parts of themselves in order to make other people (read: the dominant group) comfortable. I've been in the startup world for more than a decade and have been caught in the crossfire of a nerf pellet, a rubber band, and various startup swag in physical offices at multiple companies. I've never once been hit by anything while working remotely.

We're all dealing with a lot, all the time, whether it's a global event or in our personal lives, in addition to stress at work. Try to be understanding of your people's personal needs and schedules and create a communication culture where people can voice if they need to move a meeting due to a personal obligation. People won't do it unless they have to. If you let people be the leaders of their own lives and schedules, they're more likely to be happier, healthier, and do their best work. But, even if it didn't make them overall more productive (it does), it's just the right thing to do.

EMBRACE FEELINGS WHILE ESTABLISHING HEALTHY BOUNDARIES AROUND HOW YOU DEAL WITH THEM

Feelings are information. Strong emotions can be normal in the startup world, and dealing with them in a healthy way is what differentiates a healthy culture from an unhealthy one. If you hide your feelings, know that your team will notice.

"Vulnerability matters because we're really good at picking up on fakeness, especially in our leaders," says Liz Fosselien and Mollie West Duffy in their book *No Hard Feelings: The Secret Power of Embracing Emotions at Work.*[3]

Fosselien and West Duffy share the view that it's important to "be selectively vulnerable." This is because, especially for under-represented leaders, sharing too much can cause stress for reports, whereas not sharing at all can also cause friction, because people can tell you're hiding something.

Coach, investor, and operations leader Julie Penner recommends "red–yellow–green" check-ins. Teams can talk about how they are doing in a color scheme, without necessarily divulging the ins and outs of how they are doing or "oversharing" details beyond their comfort. This makes it safe to share the context of how individuals are doing in real-time so that teammates can take into account other factors that might affect the way someone is showing up. It's like a water gauge for how strong the current is underneath the ice.

DEFINING SUCCESS AND TRUE OWNERSHIP

Matt Harada, startup leader, and former startup CEO, drew a chart for me once: it had a large circle with many circles inside.

Divide the Pie by Startup CEO Matt Harada

Things that need to get done

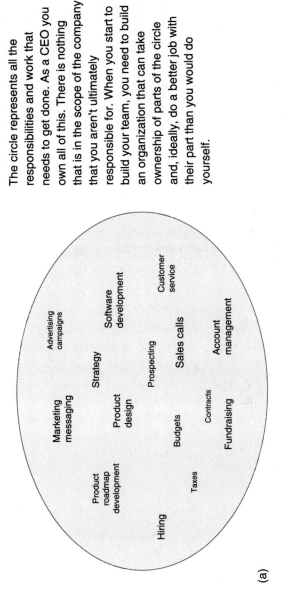

The circle represents all the responsibilities and work that needs to get done. As a CEO you own all of this. There is nothing that is in the scope of the company that you aren't ultimately responsible for. When you start to build your team, you need to build an organization that can take ownership of parts of the circle and, ideally, do a better job with their part than you would do yourself.

(a)

As CEO, I built up a team with a person responsible for each of the major areas of the business. I found myself with an appropriately sized team but still with a ton of tactical work. When I looked at where I was spending my time, it was clear that tasks in the gaps between the functions on my team were mostly landing on me.

As a former individual contributor with an executional bias, I was not holding my team to the same standard of ownership that I was holding myself. The result was that I was neglecting the higher level responsibilities that were easier to put off in favor of jumping into the latest fire fight.

There is a lot of work between the functions

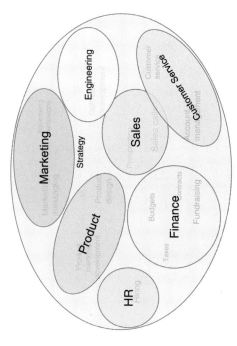

(b)

Real leaders expand into the gaps

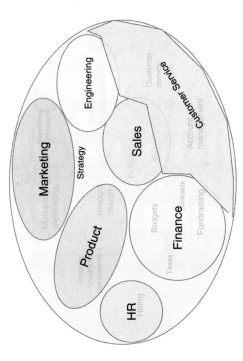

(c)

For example, finance had signed off on a customer contract template and sales were great at sending it out to prospects, but when big potential customers wanted to change the business terms, it wasn't clear who should handle that so I always got involved—even for small deals.

In the functions where I had a really strong leader, there was no gap between functions, in fact, there was overlap. There was no question of "is this my responsibility?" The leader would work with whichever of his peers needed to be involved until the problem was solved.

Once I understood that, it wasn't too hard to solve it. It took a combination of **empowerment** (e.g., Sales you need to be responsible for getting the contracts right), **trust** (Oh no, what if Sales just gives the customer whatever he wants), and some **protocols** (deals over $X need finance signoff) to keep some safeguards and make sure I was in the loop where appropriate.

The biggest hurdle was my own control tendencies. I had to be ok with taking a chance on my team and letting them make mistakes. Getting them get out of their comfort zone was ultimately better for everyone.

Fully empowered team owning the big picture

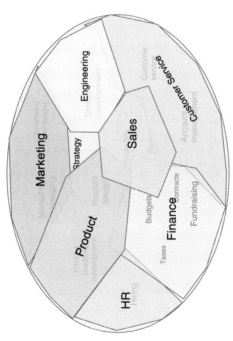

(d)

Applies up and down

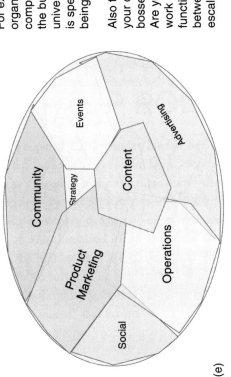

(e)

For executives, think about your own organization this way. At small companies, you may not have the budget to fully allocate your universe, but make sure your time is spent on intentional areas rather than being the default do-er.

Also think about how you and your department fits into your bosses universe of responsibility. Are you leaving gaps or can you work constructively with other functions to solve the problems in between functions without escalating them.

"As a leader, when everyone owns little pieces, you can see all of the gaps in between," says Harada. "What you want is to move to a pie ownership model, where everyone on the team owns their slice, and there isn't any space in between. As a leader, that's what will enable you to scale."

GET YOUR REPORTS TO THINK LIKE OWNERS

To the degree you're able to within your startup's culture, sharing context helps align people to perform at their best and helps them understand decisions. In your 1:1s and team meetings, share the context you have from all of your cross-functional meetings and board-level awareness (while being careful not to share things you're unable to).

A NAVY VETERAN SHARES THE CASE AGAINST COMMAND AND CONTROL LEADERSHIP

Dave Cass, Head of Partner Development at Techstars, lecturer at the University of Colorado Boulder—Leeds, and former founder of Uvize, a Techstars company that supports veterans, began his leadership journey while in the Navy. In that environment, leadership could literally mean the difference between life and death. An incorrect move could cost people their lives. That's a lot more pressure than most startup leaders face, but it set the stage for Cass' journey to be a lifelong student, mentor, and mentee of leadership.

Cass' tenure as an officer in the military helped him see that leadership had little to do with title. Title may define authority, but it has almost nothing to do with respect.

Cass says that the "command and control" leadership style, of telling your reports what to do and giving them orders, isn't even best practice in the military, counter to what some may assume.

"In the military, just giving orders is the lowest form of leadership. To lead well, you need to earn people's respect," says Cass. "When you show respect, regardless of rank, other people respect you."

Cass says when he's promoting leaders on his teams, he looks for those who are respected by their peers, as well as those who work below them on the hierarchy.

"When peers respect someone, you know, it truly is earned and it's genuine," says Cass.

HAVE YOUR TEAM'S BACK

We've all worked for leaders who were quick to throw us and our work under the bus when things weren't going well, and who took full credit for our work when things were succeeding. Cass says he coaches his students and teams at Techstars not to do this.

"I see a lot of people with the self-cover instinct," says Cass. "Could you imagine a CEO saying 'that's not my problem?' Leaders take ownership and don't blame others for what's happening around them."

LET YOUR TEAM KNOW IT'S SAFE TO MAKE MISTAKES, AS LONG AS THEY LEARN FROM THEM

The psychological safety to make mistakes and learn from them is crucial to a healthy team environment. When you make a mistake, let your team know, and also let them know how you plan to learn from it and not make it again. If you cover up your mistakes, your team will learn that this is the way to do things, even if you tell them not to. Cass says his business students most often do this, and he has to help them see that "spilling the milk" isn't the problem, it's an attempt to cover it up.

"You spilled that milk. Metaphorically just own it and clean it up. I only get upset if you lie about it on my team," says Cass.

TEACH YOUR TEAM TO PROBLEM-SOLVE AND LET THEM DO THINGS IN DIFFERENT WAYS THAN YOU WOULD

Agile coach Therese Pocrnick teaches her leaders to help people embrace problem-solving. She says that this is particularly helpful with "mundane" work that can be less glamorous.

"Problem-solving is something that a lot of people can get behind, and if you layer on things like emphasizing lifelong learning, creating psychological safety for them to fail and learn, and trying things to run experiments. Those are the things that I think will keep people engaged until the next exciting thing comes along," says Pocrnick.

Pocrnick suggests that leaders communicate intent and decentralize the decision-making of the "how" of the work.

"I can't be married to how somebody does things. Just because they don't do it my way doesn't mean that it won't get us to the right conclusion," says Pocrnick.

IF YOU'RE GOING TO BE A MANAGER, DECIDE TO CARE ABOUT PEOPLE PROBLEMS

At one point in her career, Pocrnick had to decide if she wanted to be an individual contributor or people manager.

"I was deciding whether to be a principal engineer or an architect. As a software engineer, I made a choice that I liked solving people's problems," says Pocrnick.

Pocrnick's advice to new managers on her teams who aren't sure how to lead is to "put people first."

"If you put people first, chances are you'll be directionally correct," says Pocrnick.

INVEST IN LEARNING HOW TO BECOME A MORE INCLUSIVE LEADER

Many rising leaders are so focused on making a good impression or delivering business outcomes, the idea of creating an inclusive team can feel like an after-thought, especially if you're a member of a privileged group. No matter your privilege, we all have biases, and building a more inclusive and diverse team requires effort.

According to diversity and inclusion expert Jennifer Brown, "when you are the one with the power, you have a responsibility to think three steps ahead of the comfort of others, regardless of your own identity."[4] Brown suggests that to be inclusive leaders, we all have to take actions that make our teams safer and more inclusive of difference.

HAVE FUN AS A TEAM!

Build fun into your team's success plan. From icebreakers to virtual team building days, you can consciously cultivate an environment where people on your team get to know one another and have fun together to help them become more cohesive.

The fun doesn't have to be elaborate to bring your team together. Try things like:

- A group improv class.
- Virtual icebreaker activities to find out fun facts about each other.
- Playing games together (in real life or online).
- Art activities.
- Making "fun" chat channels where people can geek out on music they like, films they've seen, or favorite recipes.

PRACTICE REPAIR AND BUILD IT INTO YOUR TEAM RHYTHM

Rupture and repair are important for secure relationships. Think about a time you or someone else made a mistake and then made amends in a personal relationship; hopefully, after, your bond was stronger. The process is the same for secure teams. On your team, figure out how you're going to do retrospectives and repair and improve when things go awry. You don't need to be perfect, but you need to ensure that, when things go wrong, everyone feels heard and you're able to grow from your mistakes.

Pocrnick tells people, her teams, and the leaders she coaches that "Sometimes you have to say, 'Sorry, I didn't show up as my best self today, or at that moment,' and then focus on asking the question of what did we learn from this?"

DO RETROSPECTIVES TO ENSURE THE TEAM SHARES THEIR VOICES AND GROWS WISER

If someone on your team makes a mistake (including you), if a launch doesn't go well, if a feature bombs, if a cross-functional meeting turns heated—these things are all okay on a team that practices retrospectives and integrates insights into making the organization perform better.

"After actions" or retrospectives identify what's happened, get everyone involved to weigh in on their experiences, and then work together to figure out how to improve going forward. If you're the one responsible for why things have gone awry, you should own up to it, but the focus here isn't on individual blame, it's on the entire organization taking responsibility.

RETROSPECTIVE PROCESS (START–STOP–CONTINUE)

Time: 1–2 hours (team)

Have a member of the team, ideally the person directly responsible for the initiative, launch, or project, run the meeting and take notes in a shared document or wiki for the team to contribute to. In addition to having people potentially contribute asynchronously, do this meeting "in real-time" to repair the team dynamic and talk through the topics together.

Here's a sample retrospective agenda. Ask all team members to contribute.

- What worked well? (Continue)
- What didn't work well? (Stop)

- What do we want to do differently next time? (Start)
- Are there unresolved topics, requests, or feelings we need to address as a team? (I add this to ensure everyone's voice is heard and to re-establish psychological safety as a team after a rupture. This may require another meeting.)

After a recent retrospective on a topic that was sensitive to many on the team, several team members shared with me how grateful they were for the process. They seemed lighter and happier after discussing what was on their minds. Doing the retro can seem daunting, but *not* doing it creates a buildup of unresolved tension in your organization. Let your team make the most of learning and give them a chance to correct and grow, and you'll go far to set the stage for a high-performing team.

PART IV

MANAGING YOURSELF AND YOUR EXECUTIVE COMMUNICATION

CHAPTER FOURTEEN

Level Up to Scale with Your Startup

As your startup grows, you'll need to scale your impact. Don't let the past you get in the way of the future you.

Upskilling continuously will enable you to expand your impact and increase the value you provide to your startup. While there will always be more to learn, embracing a process for your growth can make a big difference over time and lead to better outcomes at your startup.

MAKE AN INVENTORY OF THE THINGS YOU'D LIKE TO WORK ON

Whether you're a first-time startup executive or have been one for years, there will be things you need to learn and work on. No matter how much you've prepared (even reading books like this one), the demands of a fast-growing business require constant growth and learning. By increasing your skills across key areas, you'll contribute more value to your company, and become a more effective leader.

First, assess your current leadership style and skills. Nils Vinje, Customer Success executive and leadership coach, recommends his mentees and clients take a baseline assessment upon starting a new role or beginning a new growth course.

Identify growth areas by assessing your current skills in the following areas:

- **Tactical skills in your functional area.** VPs of marketing, sales, product, and others will outsource a lot of the execution, but we still need to understand our program on a tactical level. While you likely won't be (or stay) the Salesforce admin if you're the VP of Sales, knowing how and why sales ops has configured the instance a certain way makes you a stronger leader on the strategic level. If you don't know how to perform in a key area of your role, like building a budget, for example, you can hire a coach to train you on this or convince your CEO or CFO to find time with you. Sometimes it's useful to work with a coach who is specifically an expert in your functional area but a few years ahead of you in your career, like a CMO if you're a VP of Marketing. For example, my executive coach helped me with some of the executive-level marketing activities I needed to learn when I transitioned from "head of" to "VP of marketing" at my startup because he had deep functional area knowledge that a general executive coach or coach with a background in finance or sales might not have had.
- **Executive business skills.** Understanding how to build more effective data visualizations, how to use Excel or Sheets to manipulate data, how to build

an effective slide deck, how to organize a project well (even if that's not your role), how to write and speak effectively, are all skills you can work on.

- **Market knowledge.** Even if you're joining a field you've worked in for many years, there's always more to learn. Listen to industry podcasts, read articles and white papers. The more you can stay ahead of the curve, the better. You may notice M&A or pricing trends that you can share to inform your strategy or help define the product roadmap.

- **Customer knowledge.** This is one of my favorite areas because it's so powerful. Customers know the problems you're trying to solve intimately, and they also know the language that's effective in communicating with them (because they use it). In addition to meeting customers (virtually or IRL), it's great to listen to recorded calls between the Customer Success and/or Sales team with sales recording tools. The more time you spend with and understanding customers, no matter your functional area, the better.

- **Management skills.** Brush up on management topics like how to lead your team, hold 1:1s effectively, work through tough people challenges, and how to hire and retain talent for your team and enable them to perform. The *Harvard Business Review* and other management books like *The Making of a Manager* by Julie Zhuo and *High Output Management* by Andrew Grove can be helpful to learn the ins and outs of team management.

- **Communication and presentation skills.** Effective communication skills impact your confidence, customer relationships, cross-functional collaboration, and your relationship with your executive team. Invest in coaching or a group like Toastmasters to improve your public speaking, written communication, and slide presentations. Working with an editor or coach to improve your written communication is invaluable.

- **Self-leadership skills.** This is a big area ranging from working with your own psychology to navigating an imposter syndrome. From organizing your schedule or taking care of your emotions and psychological wellbeing at work, and learning how to lead yourself and establish effective and supportive habits and boundaries is hard but rewarding work. Getting a therapist, working with a spiritual leader whom you trust, or an executive coach who specializes in personal growth topics can be a highly useful investment that will pay dividends throughout your organization (and life).

HOW TO GET THE MOST OUT OF WORKING WITH AN EXECUTIVE COACH

Working with a coach is a powerful way to grow in your career. Here are some tips for getting the most out of working with one:

- **Look for a personal connection.** We all carry multiple identities, and our personality match with a coach is as important as any skills they could offer us. Like choosing a therapist, find someone you feel you can be vulnerable with and who you feel listens to you and is willing to help you reach your own goals, not impose an agenda on you.
- **Align your coaching work around outcomes and measurable growth.** If you're rudderless with a coach, you can spend time going in circles. While growth is often non-linear, a coach should be open to what you're hoping to achieve in your relationship together. If you're hoping for a promotion from "head of" to "VP" or "C-level," make that clear to your coach. Alternatively, if you want to become better at financial models or learn a strategic skill that your coach can help you with, make that known and find a coach willing to check in with you and give you feedback along the way.
- **Be honest and vulnerable with your coach.** If you want to show your coach only the shiny parts of your work, you'll miss an opportunity to get great help and support. Being clear about areas that aren't working or are failing is the only way to improve.
- **Use your coach to get uncommon feedback.** Your executive coach can be a great asset to your entire organization. Often, coaches will offer "360 reviews" and meet with your team and/or your CEO or boss to get and give feedback that will help you improve. If you feel comfortable with this, it's a powerful tool for your growth.

BEYOND COACHING: THERAPY IS A GREAT OPTION

Coaching is just one tool in your self-growth journey. In addition to the learning and development you do on your own, and at work, there's never been a better time to take advantage of mental health opportunities your company may offer and/or seek out resources on your own. According to San Francisco Bay Area-based psychologist Dr. Kate Ghidinelli, "when it comes to shifting maladaptive patterns that prevent us from achieving our goals or keep us stuck, working with a professional who can support you is a great asset."

YOUR GROWTH IS UP TO YOU

Your CEO, your coach, your customers, your team, your peers, and this book can all help you along your journey, but ultimately it's up to you to take ownership of your own growth. If there's something you don't know, you can learn. You don't need to know everything from day one. By committing to learning from mistakes, experiments, and from people who've done it before, you can grow yourself and your impact.

CHAPTER FIFTEEN

Leading in a Post-covid World

How do you successfully lead an organization as an executive in a post-covid world? It's not easy, but there are proven strategies that will help you stay saner and empower your teams and yourself in our new landscape.

When the global pandemic struck in 2020, the trend towards remote work accelerated. Startup leaders had yet another layer of complexity to deal with: navigating a global crisis on top of a rapid change in the work environment.

Many companies shuttered, while others thrived, particularly cloud companies as more businesses switched to remote work and people spent more time streaming at home. At the time of publishing, all companies are reconciling the impact of the crisis on their workforce and how it impacts their systems and work styles. As a leader of people at a startup, you're charged with leading with high standards, authenticity, and empathy, more often than not without being co-located with many (or any) on your team. By every measure, that's a tough thing to do.

I began a new executive role during the pandemic, and I'd only met three people in person (all prior work colleagues) for the first 18 months of my tenure. Building relationships remotely has become a skill we all need. To truly lead, no matter your office setup, you need to embrace new ways of working that meet the realities of our changing global workforce.

The Women in the Workplace 2020 report[1] published by the Lean In organization in partnership with McKinsey and Company shows "women—especially mothers, senior-level women, and Black women—have faced distinct challenges. One in four women are considering downshifting their careers or leaving the workforce due to Covid-19."[2] A study by Future Forum shows that women of color face additional discrimination and challenges working in office environments: "Office-centric work has been deeply uncomfortable for many Black workers, who are subjected to microaggressions and discrimination on the job."[3]

AS THE WORLD HAS CHANGED, PRIORITIES HAVE SHIFTED FOR MANY OF US

I recently spoke to a friend of mine who likes to call me when she is considering making a move. She hasn't made a move in four years, and is currently at a company that she enjoys, pays her well, with a team she likes.

"I have great work-life balance during the pandemic, and I like the work," she said. "But I don't know if they'll increase my compensation as fast as I'd like. This other company just offered me more money, though their culture is unknown and I am not as excited about the product."

In the past, based on previous conversations, I wonder if this friend would have optimized for money, but as we dug into her values and needs, as a single working parent, she admitted that staying at a stable job she liked that helped her achieve her other goals in life, especially during the global pandemic, was more valuable to her than a salary increase. I reflected back to her what she'd told me mattered to her, what her concerns were, as well as how she was enjoying her current role. While in the past, many of us felt pressure to keep leveling up, I'm starting to see more and more high-achievers decide that that achievement must come on their own terms.

I suspect the case may be similar for others, and can certainly identify that for me, enjoying my life and the work (and not separating the two as mutually exclusive) matters most. The discovery that she actually likes where she is and what it offers her renewed her commitment to her current leadership role.

I want to offer the caveat that it's absolutely fine to optimize for the highest compensation role you can get if that's what matters to you. (You can increase your comp *and* have a role you enjoy.) But now more than ever, many leaders are favoring roles and startups that respect our lives outside of work and enable us to lead high-performing, healthy teams. That can be worth more than roles that pay better but don't offer those qualities of life benefits.

SINCE REMOTE WORK IS HERE TO STAY, HERE'S HOW TO DO IT: IDENTIFY AND SOCIALIZE THE SYSTEMS YOU'LL USE FOR COMMUNICATION AND TRACKING WORK

Map out with your team your expectations around communication and getting work done both async and in real-time. Asynchronous tools might include wikis like Notion or Confluence; project management tools like Wrike, Asana, and Jira; CRM tools like Hubspot and Salesforce; Chat tools like Slack and Teams; synchronous tools like Slack; as well as Teams, which can be used synchronously, Zoom, hangouts, and others.

PLAN TO WORK AROUND TEAMS' SCHEDULES AND TIME ZONES

As companies become geographically spread out, identify and work around the time zones of your team and create clear expectations. Will you expect everyone to keep a Pacific or East Coast time zone, or will you have working hours where different teams overlap? Be explicit and encourage your team to block their calendars for times they're not available.

CREATE PREDICTABILITY IN YOUR OPERATING CADENCE

Operating cadence creates reliability and predictability for your team and helps people settle into a rhythm. Schedule regular team meetings at the same time each week. Try not to move 1:1s with your reports unless they do or you absolutely have to.

LEVERAGE OKRs TO KEEP EVERYONE ALIGNED

Build in explicit feedback to understand how things are going and consistently come back to OKRs to drive alignment. During weekly team and 1:1 meetings, consistently reference results and how you're tracking them. Focusing everyone on outcomes and expectations is the only way to lead when you can't possibly see everyone in an office or micromanage (and that can be a good thing!)

TAKE EXTRA TIME TO CHECK IN ON HOW PEOPLE ARE DOING

Even before the pandemic, throughout my career, I've mostly worked remotely, with some time in person. I remember early in my career, as one of the only remote employees, feeling strange when my first meeting was midday on Monday and no one asked how my weekend was. It was a small thing, but when everyone is in the office, you get an added layer of small talk and you also get the feedback of seeing people's faces and body language. When you can't see people in an office, it's hard to know how things are going. Set up 1:1s (if you use them) to create alignment and leverage Slack or another chat channel that's about social and random things because if you don't explicitly do this, it'll never happen.

SET SAFETY PROTOCOLS AND CONSIDER HIRING A COVID SAFETY OFFICER TO GATHER IN PERSON

This is a touchy subject, but depending on where you live and the state of the global pandemic in your region, gathering in-person can be challenging. To make it harder, everyone's risk tolerance and factors differ, making it more complicated to do in-person meetings. I once attended a team offsite during the pandemic where my covid safety boundaries were different from a colleague's, and we relied on the help of a third-party covid safety expert to guide all of us (thankfully!) safely through the situation. The reason is that these topics can be extra hard to navigate on our own, and can get emotional (what's more emotional than physical safety?).

If people are not comfortable gathering or if that changes for any reason based on the current state of the global or local environment, you as a team leader are responsible for creating alternative ways for engaging that don't penalize employees for keeping themselves safe at a distance. Prioritizing the safety and wellbeing of your team must always come first, and any company that skips past group safety is a red flag to look out for. If they're willing to expose you to disease for the company's bottom line, they probably are going to allow harm in other ways. Don't do this to your team, either.

JOSH ASHTON'S STORY: LEADING HIS TEAM AS CHIEF PEOPLE OFFICER AT TRINEO DURING THE PANDEMIC

According to Josh Ashton, former Chief People Officer at Trineo, during the pandemic his teams were able to come together across multiple time zones and varying pandemic realities, but it wasn't easy.

"Ironically, during the height of the pandemic, we actually got closer as co-workers. That was due to being more intentional about developing deeper relationships and connections. I think when people are in the office together, you take relationship and culture building for granted, thinking it will happen naturally, but that's not always the case." says Ashton.

Ashton recognized that his teams' priorities shifted during the pandemic.

"From a talent acquisition perspective, we noticed candidates were quick to start putting more value on how we approached talent management. Did they see that we valued results and flexibility instead of the how, when, and where the work got done," says Ashton. "Further, it emphasized the value we put on the person as a whole, not just as an employee, since they were blending more of their personal and professional lives than ever before."

Many Trineo employees are in New Zealand. The pandemic realities, especially at the beginning, were starkly different for their USA-based employees versus their Australia and New Zealand teams.

"Our New Zealand employees had actually been back in offices for quite a while before we even began to consider bringing our US and Australia teams back in," says Josh. "So everyone's challenges and realities were different. In essence, we essentially were testing out a hybrid work model where we were constantly learning how best to seek cultural and experiential parity, and at a global perspective, but then customize and personalize for local or regional situations," says Ashton. "These varying geographic realities mainly proved our theory that assuming culture and connection is stronger when you're in the office versus being remote is not always true."

REMEMBER THAT EVERYONE IS STRUGGLING WITH SOMETHING DIFFERENT

As someone who has worked remotely most of my career, working remotely in "normal times" is nothing like working remotely during a global health and economic crisis. Remember that even if someone is smiling on zoom, they may be really struggling outside of work. You don't necessarily have to talk about it, but try to remember that this is an extraordinary time that impacts everyone on your team differently. If your company has mental health or another comparable benefit, it's great to encourage everyone (including yourself) to take advantage.

CHAPTER SIXTEEN

Managing Up: How to Work with Your CEO and Board

Your success hinges on your ability to effectively manage your team and organization, but you can't do that without effective collaboration with your CEO and your board.

Relationship-building among executive teams takes time and effort. It unfolds over time and can be even harder in our remote-first world. The remote work environment presents yet another twist. For instance, my fellow executive team and I worked together for 18 months before meeting in person, and many of them had already met each other in various configurations.

In earlier chapters, we discussed the beginnings of relationship building and building relationships on your team of reports. In this chapter, we'll focus on ongoing healthy work relationships with your CEO, fellow executive utives, and board: the "managing upwards" part of leading upwards!

WORK WELL WITH YOUR CEO BY UNDERSTANDING THEIR PREFERRED WORK STYLE: FOUNDER HITEN SHAH'S STORY

According to entrepreneur Hiten Shah, in leadership roles, management goes both ways for startup leaders and their CEO.

"You're basically managing up, no matter what. You're not just managing the people that you manage, your direct reports, but you're also having to manage up. You have to manage the co-founder and CEO that are trying to manage you," says Shah.

Shah says that the way for leaders to do this well is to get to know the unique needs of their CEO or founder and work around and with them.

"There's a baseline of preferences a CEO has," says Shah. "The only way you can do that is by really understanding what their preferences are."

For Shah's reports, for example, he has a unique approach to management that doesn't involve regular 1:1s.

"Either we never have one-on-ones unless they ask for them, or we have one-on-ones where they own the agenda. Those are the two options," says Shah.

"I find people who are okay with either owning the agenda if they want the one-on-one, every week cadence, or we don't have one because they know the operating model, which is I'm always available if there's a problem, but otherwise, we won't need to meet," says Shah.

Shah admits that not every manager has his approach to OKRs. His co-founder does 1:1s and would rather have the cadence, for example.

"My model is not repeatable and you can't manage just anybody that way," says Shah. "Every CEO wants things to be different."

NOTE: YOUR CEO MAY NOT BE AWARE OF ALL OF THEIR PREFERENCES (BUT THEY STILL HAVE THEM)

Shah says that oftentimes, the people you're reporting to you as a leader in the company are unaware of their preferences.

"I am very clear about my interaction model and preferences because I have found examples of doing it my way that works extremely well," says Shah.

"But I also try to limit myself to not have that many people reporting to me unless they're managing other people, which makes this system work much better."

If in doubt, it's always a good idea to ask your CEO questions like:

- **Meeting cadence.** How do you like 1:1s to be structured?
- **Communication style.** What kind of communication should we have? Slack, Zoom calls with or without video, phone calls, text messages, or all of the above? How often should we meet in person (pending safety)?
- **Results and communication around business topics.** Do you prefer written communication like pre-read documents or slides? Do you like to get in the weeds on a call or would you prefer to high-level review major things before they ship?
- **How do you get on the same page about key information?** Do you review via email, Slack, or in a meeting?
- **What things does the CEO want to weigh in on, and how will you communicate about it?** When it comes to budget approval, review of a key initiative, or even small things like website copy, how much does your CEO want to be in the weeds and at what point will they be pulled out? It's good

to clarify if they need to see the new website hero before it launches, or if they'd prefer to just see it after the launch. As an executive, you can do many, many tactical things without "permission" because ultimately you're responsible for results, but your CEO may want to weigh in (or you'll want them to weigh in) and you should clarify what those things are and how to discuss them.

GETTING TO KNOW THE BOARD BY CONNECTING DIRECTLY WITH AT LEAST ONE MEMBER

In the early days of her startup leadership career, Broadly CEO Mindy Lauck had a "friend" on the board who could guide her into building relationships with the group and ensuring her presentations were successful.

"I had a mentor who was in the board meetings with me for the early days," says Lauck. "He was the leader I worked for in my large company prior to joining the startup, so I was very familiar with how he leads meetings and he modeled that for me. I would ask him for feedback after board meetings. Even if I wasn't leading the meeting, he would give me feedback on the section I was presenting. The relationship we had made a big difference in helping me."

ALWAYS BE CONCISE IN YOUR COMMUNICATION WITH YOUR BOARD

Gainsight CEO Nick Mehta says that many executives fail to translate the complexity of their organization and boil it down for the board audience.

"Executives take a lot of complexity and be able to translate it into simplicity, and that should show up in a smaller number of words," says Mehta. "Taking a long time to explain ideas is definitely one of the hallmarks of somebody who's new to the role."

Follow the classic (Western) business presentation method: "Here's what I'm going to tell you, I'm telling you that thing. Here's what I just told you."

NICK MEHTA'S ADVICE: FOCUS ON THE METRIC THAT THE BOARDS CARE MOST ABOUT

Boards don't want to see a laundry list of campaigns, tasks, or initiatives with their own KPIs associated. Does the board care how many website hits, how many content pieces you published, how many people showed up to your event? No. They care about bookings, sales, and customer success.

To get at the heart of how your program impacts what the board cares about, Nick shares this advice for converting your data into what the board cares about most:

- What channels did you experiment with or launch and how did that result in more growth or revenue (saved or increased)?
- Go *deal backward* vs. *lead forward*. Instead of saying how many leads converted into how many opportunities, say, out of all of the sales we had last quarter, we did $10 million sales, 45% was the result of this event we did or associated, and 25% was this white paper, etc. Work backward from the deal or the customer retention.

MANAGE YOUR TIME WELL DURING THE BOARD MEETING

During the board meeting you'll be asked questions, and be stopped throughout it. "Answer the questions quickly and concisely and then get back to the agenda so you're sure you finish on time 100 percent," says Mehta.

Mehta says the answer is inversely proportional to the length. Here's an example:

Board: "So, what was the ROI of the conference you held?"

Weak: "Well, we haven't really figured that out yet, we have to check in with the finance team, and it depends on how you look at ROI and . . . . (etc.)"

Better: "The answer is X."

Also okay: "I need to pull the exact data and will get back to you after this meeting with the answer to that question."

UNDERSTANDING WHAT YOUR BOARD REALLY CARES ABOUT

"Convince me that you're going to give me my money back at the rate of return that I want in whatever form that may take," says executive coach Gerry Valentine. Valentine says different stage investors have different risk appetites. "The investor you're attracting is different as you grow, attracting investors with a much lower appetite for risk. Your job is to deliver on their expectations and you need to seed that expectation into your organization," says Valentine.

Nicole Wojno Smith's advice for board meetings echoes Valentine's sentiment: "No one needs to see how the house is going to get built. Don't get overly detailed and tactical, especially in board meetings. The board does not need to see your 10-page marketing plan," says Smith.

A WORD OF ADVICE: DON'T OVER-PROMISE TO THE BOARD

Newer executives may promise the board the world, but this can cause headaches down the line. Remember that your board is focused on ensuring that the business is growing and will provide a return on their investment. They're interested in the bigger picture, and if you can show that you're building a program that incorporates learning and is tying its results back to the business growth objectives, you'll be many steps ahead of most startup leaders. And remember to breathe!

CHAPTER SEVENTEEN

When Things Go Pear-shaped: Navigating Challenges, Setbacks, Failure, and Departures

> *It's not always rosy in startup-land. A lot can go sideways when you're build-ing a fast-growing disruptive business in a competitive market. Here's how to navigate some common setbacks and conflicts, and advice for how to handle yourself and your organization when things go south.*

E ven when things are going well, startup life is hard. Market conditions change, a key customer churns, a competitor shifts their strategy, your app goes down, and so on. As a leader, you're expected to help your team navi-gate these changes as well as steer the ship in the right course, correcting as you go. Every day it seems there's a new challenge. While many of these will be unique to you, the types of challenges you'll face are predictable and have data-driven ways of overcoming (how to deal with missing a number, a team member quitting, a customer churning, etc.).

Knowing there are landmines won't help you avoid them entirely, but you can understand how to deal with and contextualize your experiences so you feel less alone. This chapter was one of the hardest to write, not because of lack of material (my network and I have faced many, many setbacks), but because of how endemic failure and struggle is to the startup ecosystem. It's like the water we're swimming in, so woven into how we build and grow new companies to the degree that it's almost, ironically, less visible. This, I believe, is one of the most crucial topics to address if we want to increase diversity and inclusion in the startup ecosystem. Many startup leaders internalize a narrative that everyone around me can navigate this volatility and failure, so how come I'm struggling?

The narrative goes like this: "This was supposed to be hard, but I'm having an especially hard time, so there must be something wrong with me as a leader and maybe I don't belong in the startup world."

Over-personalization of a systemic issue (startups are hard, failure happens, no one can be good at everything or anticipate everything every time) hurts everyone, but especially members of under-represented groups. Many of us have internalized that we need to be better than average (read: the straight white male majority) and to perform at a higher level, because many expect us not to succeed (even if this is unconscious), reinforcing racism, homophobia, transphobia, and other forms of systemic biases.

Who gets to "pick themselves up again" and get second and third and fourth chances after setbacks is highly related to systemic oppression. Straight cis white males I interviewed for this book had very warm and glowing things to say about times when they failed and someone "brought them back into the fold," offering them another chance, a new opportunity, or an even better job because they proved they learned from the past setbacks.

The warmth and kindness from others who'd been in the same situation allowed them to de-personalize their failures because other people did. Egregiously few women and minorities make it to the leadership level, and we see drop-offs at the seniority level for those who have made it. Studies show women over thirty-five, for example, drop out of the startup world at twice the rate as men.[1]

When we normalize difficulty and setbacks for everyone and give everyone a fair shot to try again (at least at another startup), we help the entire ecosystem. We will all experience failure if we work in startups for long enough. *All of us*, at some point. If you're a member of an under-represented group, and you fail, you deserve to continue on your path. The toxic perfectionism double-standard must not continue if we want to see more under-represented people in startup leadership. When we normalize and de-personalize the painful yet common experience of startup failures, we can see that this is part of the process and not a "problem."

If you want to be in the startup world you deserve to be here, learn and grow. This is that warm message from the universe telling you that you are so, so worthy of being here if you want to be here. You can grow from failure too, no matter your identity. Ready to dive in? Let's do this together.

LEARN TO PRACTICE COMPASSION TOWARDS YOURSELF WHEN DIFFICULTY AND FAILURE HAPPEN (BECAUSE THEY WILL)

We're all going to hit the rocks at some point on our startup voyage. All of us will underperform or face difficulty if we're in the startup world long enough.

When a person who is a member of an unrepresented group doesn't know something or underperforms in some way at a startup, it's hard to explain the weight of "it's because you were never meant to be here" (both from external and internal sources) to explain to peers in the majority. Dominant culture doesn't feature us in the roles based on the small percentages of us in the industry, so when we mess up, it can confirm that bias, rather than seeing mistakes for what they are: common mistakes.

In her book *Fierce Self-Compassion: How Women Can Speak Up, Claim Their Power and Thrive*, Dr. Kristen Neff shares that we have to be able to extend the same care towards ourselves as we do to a good friend.

"[In addition to kindness] we also need to be able to see our flaws, admit our failures, and put our own experiences into perspective," says Neff.[2]

There are areas you may have to improve to stay in your job (if you want to) or create an empowering narrative of growth and learning at your next opportunity. You can work on the areas that are being called out for competence issues without making it "true" that your competence isn't valid—at least until you find a place where it's safe to learn and make mistakes without questioning your competence or abilities as an executive.

PRACTICE SELF-COMPASSION WHEN THINGS ARE HARD AT WORK

We are human and it's normal to feel challenged when we struggle at work. We can bring compassion to the experience, acknowledging it's hard while reminding ourselves that there are other resources out there and it's okay to get help and support in forms like exercise, meditation, yoga, therapy, coaching, and talking to friends and loved ones.

"When we recognize we've made a mistake, self-kindness means that we're understanding and accepting, encouraging ourselves to do better next time . . . we stop to say 'This is really difficult. How can I care for myself at this moment?'" says Neff.[3]

UNDERSTAND THAT PEOPLE REACT DIFFER-ENTLY UNDER STRESS

Under stress, people act differently due to how human bodies are wired for survival. We have less rational, reptilian brains that are triggered into fight–flight–freeze–appease reactions. These behaviors are coping mechanisms that we evolved to help us survive. If someone is acting out of character and/or disrespectfully (including you), you can guess it's probably due to a stress reaction. This doesn't excuse any bad behavior, but it can help you depersonalize it and address the behavior while continuing to hold space for the person.

At startups (and everywhere), people's norms differ for what respectful behavior looks like. At startups, power dynamics also influence who gets to act out their stress in unhealthy vs. healthy ways. A CEO is more likely to have carte blanche with few consequences to unload stress on others than a lower-tier employee. How we all deal with our stress reactions matters a great deal to create an empowered, healthy work environment.

Examples of healthy ways to deal with stress include going for a run, doing yoga, talking to a therapist or coach, or taking a break from work to resource oneself. An example of an unhealthy way is to yell at colleagues when you're anxious or angry. Avoid the latter, and you'll be light-years ahead of most people in the startup world (unfortunately).

TREAT PEOPLE WITH RESPECT, ALWAYS

Startup leader Matt Harada goes out of his way to be kind, even (especially) when he is under stress. He values the people and relationships enough to be kind, even to those who aren't performing in a role (or sometimes are performing but their services are no longer required). He knows his limits and does his own internal work to stay calm under stressful circumstances and not project his emotions on to those around him. He can do this even when someone else is upset.

Harada has taken people out to lunch and kept great communication with folks he's let go. That's because whether or not the business relationships worked out, he still valued the personal relationships. I encourage you to be like Harada and be kind to those even as they're on their way out the door (even as you're the one showing them out). Put your energies towards regulating your own emotions so you don't expect others to absorb your stress. If you make a mistake in this arena, apologize and own up to your behavior and take steps to guarantee it doesn't continue.

WHAT TO DO IF A COLLEAGUE QUESTIONS YOUR IMPACT

The "eye of Sauron" refers to the intense scrutiny that can move from one department to another, common in the startup world. Eventually, it will come to you and your department, and your ability to deliver results will come into question. This doesn't necessarily mean that you aren't valued as a leader; it's common and it rotates around startup teams to give other teams visibility and resolve issues in departments.

The hyper-focus on your area is jolting the first time you experience it. It can come from your CEO or a peer, a cross-functional partner, like the Sales leader if you're in Marketing or the Finance leader if you're in Sales, etc. This can bring up a *lot* of feelings, especially if the delivery (context) isn't handled in a kind way.

For people from under-represented backgrounds, someone calling out our inexperience in an area we "should" know, missing a number, or being treated like "lesser than" other executives can be especially painful. It's known in Buddhism as a "double arrow" to suffer twice; the first arrow is the mistake being made and how that impacts you and the second is the additional suffering heaped on top of it by shaming ourselves or feeling bad.

Multiple times in my career, I have made a mistake comparable to or lesser than a straight white male peer of similar background and experience level. When he made the mistake, he was disciplined or had it pointed out in a neutral way (no consequences). When I made the mistake, it called into question whether I deserved to be in the role. Being a member of an under-represented group can mean we are constantly questioned for our credibility, and even the slightest mistake or lapse (or a big lapse) can prove "we weren't qualified to be here after all."

Surprisingly few people are good at giving feedback directly. Occasionally, a disgruntled colleague worried about their own success will express concerns that they feel are tied to their program and the business's success.

Some strategies for navigating negative feedback from a peer, particularly if it's not delivered to you directly:

- **Attend to your feelings.** Practice Neff's self-compassion affirmations. Get support in the form of an outside party like a coach or a therapist. Let yourself feel whatever is coming up for you, and process with an expert how this might relate to past experiences. Go for a run and eat healthy food and try some yoga and meditation. Cry, process it alone and with people outside of the company whom you trust, and try to get yourself out of an elevated or flooded emotional state where your higher-functioning brain is hijacked and back to a calmer state where you can proceed to make decisions.

- **Address the content of any concern with your colleague and/or CEO.** Once you're calmer, discuss the performance issues directly. If there are issues to resolve, talk about how you're going to resolve them (e.g., a failing area of your function may need scaling up, and here's your plan for doing that).

- **Address the context of the issue.** If information was conveyed in a way that made you feel disrespected, you need to build that working trust and address the "how" in the communication that didn't work for you and made you potentially feel bad, or even psychologically unsafe. Talk about how the context is impacting you and what your needs are.

- **Get additional data if you need to.** If you're unsure whether you're "seeing the same game" and understanding the issue you're being called out for, dig into the data and concerns so you can work together to discuss the solutions your team will implement.

- **Make requests to get your needs addressed.** Make a request to this colleague that is questioning your abilities to, say, go directly to you with feedback in the future rather than the CEO. Ask the CEO to call you with feedback vs. slacking you on the weekend, etc. If you ask for what you need, there's a higher likelihood it'll be met.

- **Make your colleague and/or CEO a part of the solution.** Make a plan, based on the data and those conversations, to fix the underperforming programs and predictably raise the numbers to hit our goals.
- **Socialize that plan with this colleague directly, first.** Model the way you want the relationship to be.
- **Share that plan with the CEO and cross-functionally, and/or to the rest of the company.** Ensure everyone understands how you're addressing the issue. Communicate the results to the leadership team and to the company, if appropriate, so everyone understands the changes made, how everyone on the team is contributing, and the impact that these efforts had on improving numbers and driving results.
- **Crush those numbers.** In the end, a colleague or your CEO raising concern about your program can help the company excel.
- **Do a retrospective.** After the content has been resolved, it's important to address context (earlier, if possible). What went well with the feedback process and what needed improvement? Were there any areas where you need to re-establish trust or build a better working relationship? How can you partner better in the future to prevent this challenge from reoccurring?

Getting constructive or negative feedback doesn't have to signal the end of your time at a company. Particularly if a colleague has gone to your boss or CEO to give this feedback without telling you first, it can be painful. In the psychology world, this is often referred to as "triangulation." While direct feedback is healthier on teams, this is surprisingly common behavior. It can be easy to sink into shame, particularly if you feel like you've been "tattled on" for some reason or that you're being questioned as to whether or not you're a true leader in your area. This often comes up in famously embattled departments like Customer Success and Sales or Sales and Marketing.

Learn from any improvement opportunities, but don't let it tell you anything about your worth in the startup world or whether you belong there. Don't let anyone else control your destiny in the startup world. At the end of the day, this is a job. There will be more jobs if this one doesn't work out.

IF YOU FAIL AND GET LET GO, OR MESS UP IN A BIG WAY, YOU STILL BELONG IN THE STARTUP WORLD AND YOU'RE GOING TO BE OK

You may fail at a leadership job, especially your first leadership job, despite trying hard and doing all the things as best as you can. It doesn't mean you weren't meant to be a startup leader. It doesn't mean you're never going to be qualified. It doesn't actually have to mean anything about the future. It means you didn't get it right this time and didn't fix it in time and so you had to go in this particular instance. You can try again, and learn from it. You are still worthy of being here.

I speak from experience when I say I've definitely felt the burning behind my cheeks when I flubbed a presentation or didn't execute something well. "I shouldn't be here," is the thought that many of us can have. Please be kind to yourself when this happens. Those thoughts can come and go, and it doesn't mean you don't belong.

WHEN YOU GET PASSED OVER FOR A PROMOTION OR A ROLE

I recently caught up with an executive candidate whom my organization didn't hire at the time. She reached out to schedule a time to chat, and I was happy to.

I didn't know her well prior to her candidacy with us and didn't have any other special relationship with her, so I was surprised that she wanted to connect.

This woman is a well-regarded leader in tech, highly experienced in her areas of expertise, and she told me she's loving her new role at a well-funded, respected, successful company. I listened, congratulated her, and we talked about our families and current events. But then all she wanted to talk about was . . . why we hadn't hired her a year ago.

She wanted to know why, what she did, and what the "real" reason was. She played the hiring decision back to me as she saw it, repeating interview outcomes and things people said. I had to jog my memory but this was all so fresh in her mind that it was like only the other day.

I was struck by her exasperation, more than a year later, regarding the decision not to give her the role. I was not the decision-maker on this hire, which she knew. After some more venting, I set a boundary and suggested that she ought to go directly to the hiring team with any questions or additional feedback.

I softened when I realized she was taking this decision very personally. I knew it wasn't personal. I knew some of the dysfunction behind the scenes. I knew that there were political reasons why someone internally was likely going to be promoted vs. bringing in someone new. I couldn't tell her any of this, it wasn't my place, but what I did tell her, this badass woman who was crushing it in her new role was this: she deserved to feel seen. She deserved to be in a role and at an organization that recognized her talents and experience, and that was excited and ready to bring her aboard to make an impact. I said I had no doubt that she would be making a very big impact in her new role and that I was excited to watch her journey.

As someone who has both not gotten jobs I've gone out for and as someone who hasn't offered candidates jobs, I know it's never easy on either side. Like in business and in relationships, it's about mutual fit. If someone or a startup doesn't feel you're the right fit, it says something about them and their needs, and not about your inherent worthiness. Try not to hold on to arbitrary decisions years later. Now go forth and find that fit (if you want!)

NORMALIZING SET-BACKS AND GIVING YOURSELF PERMISSION TO FAIL AND LEARN

Taylor McLemore, who runs Techstars Workforce Development Accelerator, says he's experienced generosity and chances to start anew after setbacks and failure. He knows this isn't necessarily something members of under-represented groups will receive.

McLemore says he once failed in a big way and felt "paralyzed." He says he sent a letter to investors, supporters, and other team members on what happened.

"I was in a very sad, dark place when I sent that letter. It was the end of something that I really believed in and cared about as a company," says McLemore.

He says the rest of the emails surprised him: they were supportive. People offered him jobs and offered to connect him with their networks, especially those who had been in his shoes before and could empathize (and see themselves in him).

McLeMore said he wished we could extend this generosity around failure to everyone in the startup ecosystem. (He is a self-identified straight white cis male.)

IS IT TIME TO CALL IT QUITS? NO ONE GETS TO DECIDE WHEN YOU STOP BEING A STARTUP LEADER BUT YOU

There are many great reasons *not* to work in startups, and no one but you knows what you need to protect your health or manage other priorities. If you want to quit the startup world, you are free to do so. The startup world can be a roller-coaster and there's no harm or shame in quitting.

I implore you: if you do want to stay, if the only thing keeping you from staying is a setback at a particular job, please know that you deserve to be here and should be here if you want to be. There are other companies with different CEOs, different founders, different customers, and different products. Don't let this one configuration or setback dissuade you from working in startups.

REFRAMING FAILURE AS ANOTHER LEARNING OPPORTUNITY

Executive Erin Rand, says there are two options: success or learning.

"Failure, really, is then an illusion," says Rand. We've all had this experience and you will too if you stay in the startup world.

Remember that no one but you gets to have the final word on:

- **Whether or not you're "cut out to be" a startup leader.** The truth is, no one is cut out to be an executive. It's a thing we made up as a society and the criteria change just as companies change and disrupt the tech landscape. If you want to be a startup leader, even if you're not "there yet," you can work on areas that are worth improving. But there's no "cut out," and certainly not that someone else could decide for you.
- **Whether you're "data-driven" or "analytical" enough.** If you struggle with being data-driven, a common issue for scaling executives, you can take online courses (many of which are free), read Cole Knafflic's book on *Data Visualization for Business Professionals* (highly recommended), hire a coach or consultant (sometimes your company will pay for this), and find other ways to learn how to become more comfortable with data.
- **Whether you're a good manager or leader.** Okay, this one can feel really bad, especially if you mess up something with a direct report. But like startup leadership, a concept made up by humans, being a good manager or leader is a skill we have evolved and can learn. If you've muddled something, you can learn from it and do it better next time.

- **Whether you have enough "gravitas" as a public speaker.** I've had plenty of people warn me I'm too shy to be a startup leader. If I'd listened to them, I'd never have experienced the joys of a flood of messages congratulating me after moderating a panel in a packed room of 1,000 people (back when we used to pack rooms in real life) at a Techstars Demo Day or speaking in front of hundreds at Lesbians Who Tech. I hired a public speaking coach. You can overcome any public speaking concerns if you want to with Toastmasters, Improv, and coaching.
- **Whether you're "scalable" as a leader (up or down in company maturity/size).** Again, there are real things to work on here to be successful in the level of execution and strategy you need to rock it at a startup leadership role. But don't let someone tell you definitively you're not scalable. If someone says "you'll never be a startup person, that's not who you are" or "you'll never scale up to grow a bigger organization" that may be true at that moment (or not!) but that's absolutely something you can work on if you want. If you choose to stay in a particular area of the startup world based on size and maturity that you're excited about, great. But don't let someone else tell you that.
- **Whether you're good enough at your function to lead it.** This may be something we all hear at some point, if only in our own heads, but remember to tell that voice that you can always improve and anything you don't know you can learn or hire around.
- **Whether you belong in the startup world!** If you want to lead at a startup, and you work hard, you deserve to be there. Period. There is no gender, sexual orientation, ethnicity, ability, age, or another external marker that determines worthiness. Just because you don't see people who look like you in the roles (yet), doesn't mean you don't belong.

It is possible that a job will end abruptly, either because of you or your employer. That doesn't mean anything has to be said and done for you and your leadership career. If you want to be a startup leader, and there's a real area to work on, you can work on it. You can try again. If you choose not to pursue a startup leadership career because it's not right for you, and you're happiest in other roles, fantastic. Go for it. But don't let someone else close the book when you're merely at the end of the chapter.

OTHER TYPES OF SETBACKS

Not Growing Fast Enough

Sometimes at a startup, you'll progress, but it won't be fast enough. Depending on your startup stage and needs, you may be under pressure to deliver or meet the needs of a pace of growth that isn't happening. That may be a failure point if you don't grow your team at the speed the business requires.

Your Department Is Underperforming (As a Whole)

If you're a sales leader and your reps are taking too long to ramp and you miss quarterly earnings projections, or you're a product leader and you miss the milestones on the roadmap, or a marketing leader and fail to deliver the pipeline or leads you committed to, those objective signs can mean an issue that's about your approach, strategy, and/or something flawed in the business model. (No Customer Success organization can make up for a bad product.)

Someone or Some Area of Your Team Specifically Is Underperforming

When we hire a team, we do our best to bring people aboard. If someone on your team is underperforming, it's your responsibility to let them know. This happens. We hire people with the best intentions, but sometimes they just aren't a fit for whatever reason. Often, it's our fault as leaders for hiring the wrong person or not helping them be successful. (No matter what, we need to take at least some responsibility for this.)

When a function that's connected to yours is underperforming, or if an entire business unit is underperforming, you could perform well but, of course, be impacted.

The Business Isn't on Track to Hit Goals and You're *Not* Responsible

Sometimes startups fail, and you had nothing to do with it. If you're in leadership, you can often see the signs quicker than your team and other employees, but there may be issues you don't have visibility into. Understand the cash position of your company, your fundraising situation, and how you're on track (or not) to meet key growth goals. But, ultimately, things happen. During the pandemic, many travel-related companies went bust and had to lay off teams. Events leaders were let go because no one was doing events in person.

The Business Isn't on Track to Hit Goals and You're Responsible

This is a tough one, and it speaks to the reason why this book exists: it is hard to be a successful startup executive. If it were easy, everyone would do it.

You Missed an OKR

Temporary lags in performance can be seasonal and/or attributed to a fundamental issue with your strategy. This is stress-inducing and difficult, but remember, it happens. If you can course correctly, ideally you can take the lessons learned from missing a number and improve the following quarter. Talk to your CEO early and often when you think you might not hit a number so you can work together to adjust the course. If you consistently miss your numbers, you may likely be let go.

OTHER THINGS THAT CAN GO WRONG AND HOW TO DEAL WITH THEM

Your Cross-functional Department Head Fails

This is surprisingly common: You're hired on as VP of marketing, or VP of sales, and your counterpart doesn't cut the mustard. CEOs and founders are taught to "fire fast" because of how stressful it is for an underperformer to stay aboard. If you're in a situation where your counterpart isn't pulling their weight, it can be challenging to identify it, and then once you identify it, know how to navigate it. Hiten Shah says that often this is outside of our sphere of influence. The important thing is to continue delivering in your area when a cross-functional partner is failing. Shah says sometimes we get emotional or caught up in trying to control a situation like an underperforming counterpart, but that patience is often the best and only way to navigate.

What To Do When a Failing Executive Tries to Take Down Your organization With Them

A failing executive may try to blame others around them in an attempt to save themselves. For this reason, the moment you realize your counterpart is slipping, be extra careful about documenting your department's contributions and ensuring your team's performance continues.

For instance, if you're in marketing, and a sales leader who's struggling is pointing fingers at the marketing organization for sales whiffing on their number, it can help to work with your Ops team to run salesforce reports that show pipeline quality, pipeline attribution (i.e., where the leads and opportunities originated from by channel/source), and also prove that marketing brought in these leads to sales accepted.

If the sales team doesn't touch the leads for 30+ days, pull reports to show that if it comes in as a question. It isn't pleasant to need to cover yourself or your program, because, ideally, your co-functional leader will be a good partner to you and you'll act as one revenue team (in this example), but expect that an underperformer may try to drag you all down in the process.

If sales says "marketing isn't bringing any good leads," you'll have metrics to help make the case. If you're in customer success and sales says "you didn't deliver the success to help them expand," have data on things like NPS and how your team is performing. And onwards. Ideally, your founder and CEO will be able to use this context to help this person who isn't performing swiftly move to another part of the business and/or out of it entirely.

Your Organization and/or Business Is Going Well But You're Burnt Out or Facing Another Personal Challenge That's Difficult

Burnout is rough, and with today's business culture, it can feel inevitable. There are many great resources out there (check out *Burnout: The Secret to Unlocking the Stress Cycle* by Emily and Amelia Nagoski). If you're burnt out, it's crucial to take time to rest and recharge. The business problems will be there for you to solve when you get back. If you're working for a startup where it isn't possible to get that, think about making a move. Your health comes first, and everything else flows from it.

Aubrey Blanche is a successful hyper-growth executive, working at companies like Atlassian and Culture Amp. In her blog post about dealing with mental health challenges, she says, "I think it's easy to tell yourself a story that if you take a little bit of time out for yourself, everything's going to come crashing down. And that's not true, even in elite, scaling, hyper-competitive startups."[4]

ADVERSITY IN THE STARTUP WORLD IS A FEATURE, NOT A BUG

According to Mike Tyson, "everybody enters the ring with a plan and a strategy and then they get punched in the face."

At some point, all startups will hit bumps in the road. A CTO will quit. A lead investor gets fired from their firm, and the new investor is no longer a champion. Lead customers churn. This is startup life.

"It's not easy," says Jeff Bussgang. "I had a note from one of my partners that one of our founders is tired and is just having a hard time pushing forward. We're all very thoughtful and sensitive about mental health and illness and energy depletion, but when entrepreneurs are tired, it's over, it's done. And so they've really got to rally themselves to keep that energy level high, then rally their teams," says Bussgang.

NAVIGATING PIVOTS SUCCESSFULLY AS A STARTUP LEADER

Along the way to "up and to the right" growth, there may be a significant change in direction, otherwise known as a pivot. The way to get through? Lots of communication.

Before their pivot, entrepreneur Hiten Shah's company raised money from investors for what they were working on prior to the pivot.

"We continued sending our regular investor updates, which were a monthly first Monday of every month at 8 a.m. investor update. No matter what period, they got sent. It's just in something (my co-founder) Marie and I both worked on that has my name on it, but we both worked on it and got it done and it's our investor update for our investors to let them know what happened that month so that they're in the know if we weren't doing that. The investors would not be on board with the pivot if we weren't doing that," says Shah.

Shah says he and his leadership team were transparent in sharing these pivot updates with everyone at the company, from the interns to the investors.

TREAT PIVOTS AS A CHANCE TO BECOME A BETTER COMPANY

Shah says they pivoted in a way that enabled the whole company and investors to have full transparency because this was the approach they knew would enable them to win.

In a pivot, as an executive, you may not have all of the information that founders and co-founders have. Take it upon yourself to find out as much as you can, share what you can with your team, and help everyone get on board with the new plan.

IN TIMES OF CRISIS, UNDERSTAND YOUR CIRCLE OF CONTROL

We all have things within our circle of influence and control and things outside of it. The "serenity prayer" in the recovery world (Grant me the serenity to accept the things I cannot change, courage to change the things I can, and wisdom to know the difference) applies well to startup leadership.

Shah says people get caught up in territory that isn't their problem or that they can even influence, and they get caught up because they're trying to control things.

"I see a lot of people driving themselves nuts, trying to control things. They don't have control in the work environment and are trying to get upset about all these things. At the end of the day, you don't control it. So then you have a decision to make. Do I stay here? Or do I not? Because that's the ultimate decision," says Shah.

According to Bussgang, "Nothing fixes morale like winning," says Bussgang. Get your team in a position to win again with areas you can control.

STAY AND ACCEPT, TRY TO CHANGE THINGS, OR LEAVE?

Shah says when someone complains to him about their job, when it's related to something they don't control, he asks them to reflect on "Are you willing to have patience here and see how it plays out? Or do you want to leave the job? Because that's not in your control."

In startups, boundaries and roles are blurred and people can impact change across an organization. The key is to consistently ask yourself in a situation if you can control it or if you can influence it.

IN TIMES OF MAJOR CHANGE, CONSIDER HAVING AN "ON THE BUS OR OFF THE BUS" CONVERSATION WITH YOUR TEAM

Executive coach Gerry Valentine talks about "on the bus or off the bus" conversations he's had with startup leaders at key moments of growth and/or pivots when it's clear that not everyone will be "coming on the bus" for the next step of the journey.

"On the bus/off the bus" conversations can re-establish company morale and that people who are not on board are moving on with the most grace possible.

Valentine says, if possible, companies can give their leaders the opportunity to make it easy to exit the business with a severance package and "part as friends" if people aren't on board with the new vision. The people who stay will be rewarded with a better work environment.

"People could easily have walked out the door and found another job. If people wanted to do that, we would wish you luck and we're doing everything we can for you. But if you want to be on the bus, you're on the bus and we're going to be as clear as we possibly can for you about what we believe that road is going to look like," says Valentine.

During pivots and difficult times, you need to have some version of that "on the bus" conversation. Startups change, and people and leaders who worked well won't either want or be able to scale immediately. Be really clear and to make it okay for people to say, "you know what, I am not on the bus" and do your best to help them transition gracefully.

IF YOU STAY, KNOW YOU WON'T AGREE WITH ALL DECISIONS

"Don't take decisions personally that are made in the context of where the business needs to go," says AQUAOSO founder and CEO Chris Peacock.

"If the thing you were working on gets fully sidelined or if the company changes, it's not a personal thing. It's very much more about what the company needs to do in order to probably stay alive. There's a lot of experimentation that takes place and hard decisions have to be made sometimes," says Peacock.

TURNING A STARTUP PIVOT INTO A STARTUP LEADERSHIP ADVANCEMENT OPPORTUNITY: MINDY LAUCK, CEO OF BROADLY

Mindy Lauck, CEO of Broadly says: "I was at a large company for a long time and a mentor of mine left and convinced me to join a startup with him. So I was excited to go back into startups," says Lauck. "I joined the team to completely reimagine and rethink the product experience. So it was a pretty major shift. We changed everything, going from a free product to a paid subscription. It really was a different entity by the time the product that the founder had created was produced and it had worked like that for many years. It was a true pivot."

Lauck was in charge of the strategy, but the product ended up driving the whole company. Lauck identified that the product strategy in the company strategy "weren't so far apart."

The next thing she knew, Lauck was in all of the board meetings because the product was the focus, and it had started gaining in revenue and market share.

"I was running the board meetings eventually, because that's where the focus was," says Lauck. "There was one moment in a board meeting, where I was the CEO. The co-founder kicked off the board meeting and probably spoke for about two minutes and then the rest of the meeting was mine. We didn't actually speak about it at that moment, but things started to feel different," says Lauck.

During the pivot, when Lauck stepped up to lead the company in a new direction, she was made CEO. She credits her ability to be adaptable and provide value during the pivot as crucial to her leveling up to CEO. If your business is going through a pivot, you may have an opportunity to expand your role or provide additional value along the way.

DON'T TRIANGULATE: IDENTIFY "YOU TWO" PROBLEMS

To the degree possible, let your team work conflicts out together rather than being a go-between. When a vision or mission is unclear, or goals need to be realigned, you can jump in, but if you're constantly interfering in interpersonal relationships, that causes your team to expect you to do that.

If you or someone on your team is talking about a third party in the company who is not in the room at the time, if you can, bring them in the room and encourage the two people to talk. As a leader, managing people, you can help establish this practice. When Hiten Shah finds himself recommending something like: "Say, I'm happy to facilitate if you want, but this is a 'you two' problem. This is not a 'me' problem, right?" In many cases, a timely, direct conversation will be the most efficient solution and save everyone from unnecessary go-between drama.

ON THE FAME/ BLAME CYCLE—WHEN THE HIGHS ARE HIGH AND THE LOWS ARE LOW

There is a Buddhist principle about the cycle of "blame/fame," meaning that we experience both as temporary states. Getting caught up in either can cause suffering. While we often talk about the highs and lows in the context of entrepreneurship, we don't frequently discuss it in the context of startup employees. We absolutely feel the rollercoaster of startup life. Know that the lows are part of the journey and normalize them with your team.

DEPARTURES: WHEN IT'S TIME TO MOVE ON FROM YOUR ROLE

In *The Alliance*, authors Reid Hoffman, Ben Casnocha, and Chris Yeh frame jobs as "tours of duty." Today, few jobs are meant to last forever (or through retirement, at least) and one day you'll need to be prepared for when it's time for your startup leadership role to end—either by your choice or the company's.

When it's you making the decision to move on, you'll need to manage the process differently than when you were a manager or even a director. There are different expectations about timing, including how to ensure that the transition of leadership goes smoothly. When you were an individual contributor, you could leave with the confidence that it was "someone else's problem," whereas as an executive, you're generally expected to be more involved in the transition process.

DECIDING WHEN IT'S TIME TO MOVE ON

The decision when to leave a role is hard. You've put time and energy into being successful. Likely, you've got unvested equity. You may still believe in the mission. Or, perhaps you don't and you no longer believe in the company direction.

QUESTIONS YOU CAN ASK WHEN DECIDING WHETHER TO LEAVE YOUR EXECUTIVE ROLE

- Do you need to change something, and if that thing could change, would you want to stay?
- Do you just need a break or a holiday?

- Is there something fundamental going on where it's not the right match anymore?
- Do you no longer feel aligned with the company mission or direction?
- Is there another role or opportunity that's more aligned with your goals or mission at this stage?

If you do feel it's time to move on based on these answers, and you're ready, here's your plan.

HOW TO LEAVE A ROLE LIKE AN EXECUTIVE

First things first: Forget everything you know about the famed "giving two weeks' notice".

"Giving two weeks would be horrifically unprofessional at an executive level when you have that level of responsibility," says startup executive Erin Rand. "At the VP level, I can't even imagine someone coming in on a Monday and saying 'I'm out of here next Friday.'"

If not two weeks, what's the standard as a startup leader? Typically, thirty days is the minimum amount. In some cases, you might offer to extend that on your way out, depending on your ability and willingness to do so. You might stay to finish a critical project or to cover while the company replaces you since startups don't have a bench of talent that a larger company does. People already have a lot on their plates, so your leaving will make an outsize impact. Plus, there are considerations like ensuring your team is set up for success, the critical projects are transitioned, and you're leaving the company in a good place. Usually, if you're headed to a new place, they'll willingly wait for you.

"I recently hired a new general counsel, and we waited the other side of three months for her because in her previous role, there were major projects, initiatives, and things to finish up. They were in the middle of an acquisition. We were willing to wait for her," says Rand.

HOW TO GIVE NOTICE

This will depend on the relationship you have with your CEO and/or the person to whom you report. If you're very close, you may have even discussed what a potential departure could look like. While it may be tempting to storm off or depart with a trail of trash can emojis in a Slack thread, leaving with the least drama possible is the best approach, in most cases.

"At a former company, my CEO and I had an agreement that if one of us didn't think it was working out anymore, we would promise to tell each other and create a great plan for the departure," says Rand. "When I finally did give that notice, I just had to tell him 'the day has come'."

If you haven't set the stage for a departure, that's okay, it's not the only approach. You'll need to have a conversation with your manager. Tell them you're planning on leaving, when you'll be available until, and start the process of creating communication, transition, succession, and other "off-boarding" tasks. It is common for people to immediately follow up with this meeting with a written notice outlining the key facts via email.

WHEN YOU GIVE NOTICE: BE PREPARED TO BE ASKED TO CLOSE YOUR LAPTOP ON THE SPOT

When you give your notice, you may offer a thirty- or sixty-day transition period. You're ready to roll up your sleeves and prepare to leave smoothly, and then . . . your CEO tells you to close your laptop after the meeting or call. You're done. This may sound harsh but you should be prepared for that scenario. It does happen, so it's worth mentioning. If you can't afford to be out that day for any reason, you may need to plan when you choose to give notice. Some startups are afraid of people stealing Intellectual Property (IP), the impact someone leaving who's still around could have on morale, a personal grievance, and so on, so they want to "walk them out" right away.

The best advice here is to look at how other executive departures have gone at your startup. Does the CEO blow up and force them out the moment they give word? Alternatively, does the company typically work with the departing leader to create an action plan that allows for flexibility around timing and a joint under-standing that the transition will be a gradual and mutual one? You'll have a sense also for how firings go: are people let go immediately that day or do they get a bit of breathing room to wind down projects? Often, companies put severance language in hiring contracts, so this is another area to read closely in your offer.

A WORD OF ADVICE: RESPECT THE COMPANY'S INTELLECTUAL PROPERTY (IP) AND DON'T TAKE IT UPON DEPARTURE

This is a strange piece of advice, but here it is: don't take company files after you decide to leave. That looks bad, even if you don't plan to use them and you intend to put them in an ice vault forever and never look at them. (I assume this is where mediocre slide presentations go once they pass on to the next life, but I digress.) Your "why" doesn't matter. You don't want to create any situation upon leaving that could be construed negatively or harm the company. In the event of any kind of legal situation down the line, if you end up getting a role at a competitor (even years later), you don't want that kind of liability. It's not worth it. Be respectful of the company's IP, and know that the lessons and knowledge you've gained will stay with you forever.

ANOTHER WORD OF ADVICE: BE CAREFUL ABOUT POACHING EMPLOYEES (AT LEAST RIGHT AWAY)

Many companies include contracts about poaching employees. Check your contract and be sure to honor it. This mostly applies to taking entire departments (think siphoning an entire sales team from the current company and plugging them in at your new company), but you need to check your legal terms and be careful. There are many schools of thought on this topic, and you'll find conflicting advice, but in my perspective, this is a very long game (hopefully) and people will remember how you treated their company upon leaving. If you take the star employees with you, they're not going to take it lightly, so know you're going to potentially burn bridges.

EXERCISING YOUR VESTED EQUITY AROUND YOUR DEPARTURE

Any unvested equity generally goes away (poof!) when you leave a company. Sorry. But the vested equity options you haven't yet exercised (if you have them) present a choice: do you exercise your shares? You will only be able to do so within the window—usually a highly limited period after you leave—so check your equity terms and consult a lawyer. Sometimes, you can negotiate an extension on your equity vesting period, so if you're concerned about being able to come up with enough cash to buy your equity, it's worth discussing with a lawyer or a tax advisor and then seeing if that could be discussed with your founders.

TAKING TIME OFF IN BETWEEN JOBS

Startup leadership is enervating, and you'll benefit from taking time off (at least a few weeks, more if you can financially accommodate it) between roles to recharge, re-set, and explore life outside of the office. "I've never seen anyone regret taking time off in between roles," says startup executive Erin Rand.

Many executives take time off between roles, so if you are financially able and decide to do this, know that it's not something future hiring committees would likely ding you on (if that's a potential concern). Many executives decide to leave their current roles not because they're "running" from their current jobs, but because they have a new exciting opportunity lined up. In that case, you likely have a new job offer and will need to balance the departure process at your current company with your new role's timing.

MAKE A COMMUNICATION PLAN

When people join startups, there's a sense of camaraderie and alignment around a disruptive mission. When a key person leaves, messaging becomes more critical than ever. It's important to be a part of the story of why you're leaving or others at the company will be negatively impacted.

You need to figure out with your CEO how you're going to deliver the news, and what the plans will be for helping your team and other cross-functional partners manage the transition.

KEEP IT POSITIVE

"Tell the positive story, and there has to be truth in it," says Rand. "Sometimes you're leaving because you're burnt out, sometimes you're leaving because you don't believe in the mission anymore. For gosh sake, don't leave a void and say nothing, because people will fill in the blanks in the story and it will often not be a good one, because people will have anxiety whenever a leader is leaving," says Rand.

"You can't leave gracefully while assigning blame," says Rand.

If you've truly decided the company can't keep you, talking about what's wrong won't solve anything. After all, you're not going to change things, you're out the door, and the company is unlikely to make those changes because you said them as you left. That being said, if there are valuable insights you can provide on your way out the door that show you're still invested in the company's success, feel free to provide them. If you make sure big things don't fall off the table, that's great. Don't make it an excuse to dump on the company on your way out. After all, every startup has its flaws, and the things you didn't want to work through or deal with anymore will become someone else's challenges soon.

BEWARE THE "DILBERT PRINCIPLE" AND LEAVE WITH GRACE ANYWAY

Erin Rand describes what she and her (also a techie) husband Ray call the "Dilbert Principle": when you leave a company, for the next six months, everything that goes wrong is going to be your fault.

"It's the easiest thing in the world to just put that on the shoulders of whoever's not in the room anymore. It's not personal, and I don't think people do it intentionally," says Rand.

While you can't control this phenomenon after you leave, do your best to leave as gracefully as possible.

PART V

PROVING, SUSTAINING, AND EXPANDING YOUR IMPACT AS A LEADER

CHAPTER EIGHTEEN

Measuring Success: How to Know If Things Are Working

How to connect your activities to business growth and report on your performance at the executive level. Plus, how to get feedback about areas for improvement.

Connecting your department's activities and programs to business growth by measuring and reporting on the key performance indicators is a crucial aspect of your role as a startup leader. The real mission here is to bring a story to the data. No one cares about every single data point on your team, especially not your board. We've talked about how to report at the board level, linking the most important metrics in your department to business results. In this chapter, we focus on the leading and lagging indicators in your program.

WHO CARES ABOUT LEADING AND LAGGING INDICATORS?

Leading indicators are the gates on the downhill ski run that show you're hitting your marks and will have a successful finish. If you miss one, you may miss the big indicator. Tracking the leading indicators will allow you to course-correct early, before something impacts your revenue, churn, or another growth number.

The lagging indicators are those numbers that usually make it onto your objective and key results (OKRs) slides. Leading indicators usually have a strong, quantifiable relationship to lagging indicators, meaning if you generate X% growth of one leading indicator, you can predict Y% growth of the lagging indicator.

Examples of **leading indicators** and their **associated lagging indicators**:

- **Marketing.** Marketing qualified leads (MQLs) volume as a leading indicator influencing the lagging indicators of marketing opportunities generated and marketing pipeline.
- **Customer success.** Product usage is a leading indicator for customer churn or net revenue retention (NRR).
- **Sales.** Meetings booked per rep per week is a leading indicator affecting pipeline closed per rep per quarter.
- **People ops.** Initial candidate interviews conducted per week is the leading indicator for hired candidates per quarter.

UNDERSTANDING THE METRICS THAT SET UP YOUR DEPARTMENT FOR SUCCESS

If you're the VP of People, the board certainly doesn't care about every metric your Applicant Tracking System (ATS) generates. Your CEO probably doesn't either.

They do care whether time-to-fill in roles has decreased and the quality and retention of candidates has improved because of the strategy you've implemented.

FOCUS ON MEASURES THAT SHOW OUTCOMES VS. ACTIVITY

Key performance indicators can provide objective insights for your own team, your cross-functional peers, your CEO, and the board into the performance of your areas and opportunities for improvement. Instead of focusing on the number of accomplishments (e.g., we hosted four events, 250 people came, etc.), talk about how much pipeline revenue you generated and what percentage of your goal Events and Field Marketing brought in.

When you care about the leading indicators that matter most, you can share this level of detail with other teams to help tell the story of your journey to success:

- A marketing leader can share the numbers that contribute to the ultimate goal of pipeline closed (closed revenue brought in from marketing).
- A sales leader can show the increase in outbound meetings their reps are booking as leading indicators they're on the path to closed–won deals.
- A customer success leader can show the increased usage they're driving through success activities and how that leads to lower churn and higher net revenue retention (NRR).

GETTING COMFORTABLE WITH QUANTITATIVE MEASUREMENT TOOLS

Depending on your background, quantitative measurement might be intimidating. Many first-time Sales and Marketing leaders I spoke to had to take courses, get coaching, and do intensive study to feel confident working in spreadsheets and telling stories around the data and results. The good news is that, especially on go-to-market teams, revenue operations and other professionals can help you pull data from your various systems to track the KPIs you care about. You won't be alone in telling the story. You may want to hire a dedicated Ops person on your team to support your success.

Quant tools to get comfortable with:

- **Dashboards.** CRM and customer data platform tools can offer a snapshot into the KPIs that matter and track them over time.
- **Spreadsheets.** Every startup still uses them, at least for some tracking. If you ever think "I wish we could do x outside of a spreadsheet," it either (a) already exists as a tool you can buy or (b) is a tool that should exist and you could build it in a startup. So much is still surprisingly manual, even at the time of writing, but tools like Zapier and other integrations can automate some of your reporting into spreadsheets. If you get stuck, an operations consultant or agency can help you get your spreadsheet in order. Online courses at Udemy and Coursera are also great options to improve your spreadsheets acumen.
- **Scorecards.** For hiring and candidates, creating a list of the metrics stack-ranked by priority helps you avoid bias and track how individuals you're thinking of hiring are performing against traits that matter.
- **Data visualization.** Tools like Tableau and other similar platforms can be useful for tracking trends. Also, read Cole Knafflic's book *Storytelling with Data* and get comfortable making visualization language part of your reporting.

HOW THE BOARD THINKS ABOUT YOUR INDICATORS

Investor Jeff Bussgang says that churn and revenue are lagging indicators that he often looks out for upstream.

"When a customer is unhappy, certain things happen and then they reliably churn," says Bussgang. "You want to look at the leading indicators, which are more like usage or net promoter score or number of logins and time on task and time in the app. Those are all leading indicators of happiness with a product and the customer, as opposed to the lagging indicators of the churn."

MEASURE WHAT COUNTS AT A REGULAR CADENCE

As you regularly measure what counts for your department week-over-week, month-over-month, quarter-over-quarter, and so on, form an opinion on the *why* behind the data.

OTHER "SUCCESS" MEASURES

Your startup will need to measure and report on to your CEO (and the board, depending on the stage) factors including:

- Summary financials.
- Product roadmap.
- Sales pipeline.
- OKR attainment.
- What went well since the last board meeting.
- What did not go well and how the business plans to fix it.

If the charts are all up-and-to-the-right, that's great, but do you know why? What channels are performing best in marketing, and what investments should you make next to scale results? What sales outbound techniques are working and which do you need to cut? The point of startups is to learn quickly. Those who can launch quickly, interpret results, and use data to inform future actions are successful. If you wait too long or aren't looking at the data closely, you'll miss opportunities.

LETTING LEADING INDICATORS GUIDE YOUR EARLY-STAGE STARTUP GROWTH

On the go-to-market side, we talk about understanding our pipeline with "deal backwards" vs. "lead forwards" perspectives. We tell the story about revenue won vs. looking just at what we're doing without seeing its eventual result. It sounds obvious, but you'd be surprised at how many leaders get confused by the two. Vanity metrics are insights that look great on paper but don't necessarily translate to results.

For example, "Hey, we got website traffic from 100 candidates for our open role this week!" is fine, but does it translate into things that really count? How many of those 100 candidates turned out to be good-fit applicants? How quickly did you fill the role? To make it even simpler, if you report that your BDR team sent 1,000 emails that week but none of them were opened or clicked by a prospect, that's an example of a vanity metric vs. one that has real leading indication (clicked BDR emails translating into a meaningful conversion to demo meetings booked, etc.).

Other financial metrics that investors at modern SaaS companies look for:

- What is your revenue?
- What's your margin?
- How much leverage are you getting in terms of your capital deployed?

Founders and startup executives need to be fluent in those topics, but in the early days they need to maximize learning over financial metrics.

"I don't care if your revenue is zero and stays zero for two years, if you're learning a lot, and can show how what you're learning is contributing," says Bussgang.

RAND FISHKIN'S ADVICE FOR METRICS: KEEP IT SIMPLE

Entrepreneur and marketing expert Rand Fishkin advises looking at two or three metrics that matter.

"It may surprise some to find out that when it comes to the metrics that count, I like to keep it as simple as possible. I think that there's a ton of obsession, especially in marketing, with KPIs and multiple metrics and ways of measuring. *Here's our brand impact from this PR campaign. Here's our search impact from this campaign. Here's our content impact from this campaign.* Many folk who are obsessed with the measurement at those granular levels are going to spend a huge amount of their effort over-investing in channels that produce measurable results, rather than useful and best results in the metrics that count most," says Fishkin.

HOW TO WORK WITH YOUR CEO ON MEASURING YOUR PERFORMANCE

As you set OKRs, confirm with your CEO the most important metrics you'll report on. For example, my marketing organization might commit to $X million in opportunity pipeline from marketing sources and X opportunities. *Many* leading indicators roll up to these two numbers (and indicate whether or not we'll be successful), but that's not the level of detail I commit to. If my CEO wants to see in the weeds (which we do), it is documented, but that's not how I manage the business. The CEO doesn't care how many demo requests are filled out each week or how many website visitors we have so much as how much pipeline we generate that's closing into meaningful ARR for the business.

"As CEO, when it comes to the metrics you manage in your business, you decide. It's not up to me to tell you. Your job is to measure these things," says Fishkin.

"I think in a healthy organization you are leaving that to the experts and the experts should be your VPs or C-level executives who work for you. And if you don't trust them to make the decision about which thing to measure, that was probably the wrong hire or you're a terrible manager," says Fishkin.

BUILDING ACCOUNTABILITY INTO YOUR TEAM REPORTING

Everyone on your team should know which metrics they drive that contribute to the larger goal. For example, the sales team should know how their booking meetings with their SDR contributes to their successful quota attainment.

CHAPTER NINETEEN

Communicating Your Results to Your CFO, CEO, Company, and Board

You've defined and achieved success. Now it's time to tell the world. Learn how to present your results to your leadership organizations in the most common executive presentations, from all-hands, to QBRs, to Board Meetings, and understand the why behind all of these activities.

The first time I presented in front of a board, I had prepared with my executive coach and submitted slides to my CEO in advance. I showed my function's (marketing's) performance, learnings, and our organizational growth plans for the next quarter. I labeled the results to show what was working and what we planned to improve going forward.

The board members said nice things. We'd grown quarter-over-quarter since joining, and marketing had 10 times more results since I'd joined. Great, right? I was feeling pretty confident. Then one of our board members asked: "Why are my other portfolio companies growing faster than you?"

My CEO ended up fielding that question. It was fine and we moved on, but I'll never forget the sinking feeling I had and the visceral understanding that board meetings were a totally different ballgame than QBR presentations internally. While this nerve-wracking first-time experience was challenging, it taught me that (a) board meetings are a thing I can do and (b) boards are looking for "across the board" insights.

WHY BOARD MEETINGS EXIST (AND NO, THEY'RE NOT JUST TO TORTURE STARTUP FOUNDERS AND EXECUTIVES!)

Your board wants a return on their investment in your startup. They've seen startup founders and executives miss goals before, and that's not necessarily going to phase them. Through board meetings and other board-level communication, they aim to understand how your business is growing, what insights you're applying in order to accelerate growth, and where the team is performing (or not). They want to validate their assumption that this business will generate a return. Boards "pattern match" for a living and can smell B.S. from a mile away.

"The board is there because they want you to succeed, because when you succeed they succeed," says startup executive Rachel Beisel.

COMMUNICATING AT THE BOARD LEVEL

Boards want you to be honest with them and take responsibility for your failures in addition to your successes. They also look at how your company is performing against their other investments, and your likelihood to give them an outsize return and "return the fund". Meeting with them regularly in order to update them on all of the above has become a ritual in our industry that frankly can scare off many would-be startup leaders.

Lack of representation at the board level is a barrier to more inclusive startup leadership, because presenting to a room full of folks who all look the same and not like you can be intimidating. (It's probably intimidating even if you *do* look the same as the board!) So let's demystify these meetings and communications and unpack what's necessary to execute them well.

COMMUNICATING AT THE "ALTITUDE" OF THE BOARD

It's easy to get tunnel vision around your own department. Board-level communication and strategy is one of the biggest shifts that you'll have to make as you grow in your executive role. For example, a marketing leader cares about every piece of content, every account-based marketing campaign, and each event. The board wants to know not just how a program performed, but why you ran programs, and how you can prove that running programs is the right strategy in terms of increasing business revenue or growth. The results you deliver must be shared in the context of their impact on business success and how the kinds of programs or projects you're running are working. It's not just "We will hire four great sales reps." It's "we are confident that scaling our reps to four with a $1.5 million per year quota will put us on pace to achieve our revenue targets this year."

HOW IS YOUR BUSINESS PERFORMING WITHIN THE CONTEXT OF THE GREATER MARKET (OR THE VC'S PORTFOLIO?)

Remember that VCs are looking at how you're performing, not just in your own right but within your cohort (similar companies in your market) and their portfolio. Many VCs won't push the business to become a Unicorn or bust within a tight time-frame, but they are looking for companies that can deliver them an outsize return, so they can go back to their limited partners (LPs) and successfully raise their next fund.

The good news is, regardless of whether you have a value-add board of investors who truly care and want to help and won't push your founding team towards their own agenda, you have control over how you perform in board meetings. It's within your control to give the meetings the most value possible and empower your boards to understand an accurate picture of how things are going, and hopefully provide value.

Board meetings will evolve as your startup grows. At the early stage, your founders may have informal syncs with the board discussing high-level metrics (how's our burn and/or churn, are we growing ARR, have we made key early hires, etc.?). These will become more structured as the company scales. Public companies run board meetings like tight ships due to the transparency required for shareholders. *Startup Boards* by Brad Feld is a great resource to understand investor and CEO perspectives on board topics.

Here are some tips for effectively communicating your results to your board and startup shareholders.

DO YOUR HOMEWORK

Understand who is on the board. Is it a "friendly" board of mostly the founders' friends, and/or are you at a stage of growth where investors from multiple

VC firms are present? Are there "observers?" Which founders are on the board? Find out also the board members' backgrounds and industries so you can come prepared for the types of questions they'll ask. For instance, many board members have finance backgrounds, so getting your CFO-level reporting for your department tight is helpful.

BUILD RELATIONSHIPS WITH THE BOARD PRIOR TO YOUR FIRST MEETING

"As you build a relationship with them, get a sense for where some of their blind spots are," says Matt Heinz.

"Only three to four percent of board members have marketing experience. Every person on the planet thinks they know how to do marketing. So you may have a board member who is thinking about your business once a quarter who has never done marketing. They may feel like they have to have a comment on your marketing strategy because they're on the board when they're just making it up as they go. So, you need to contextualize your presentations and understand where their expertise is depending on your role," says Heinz.

TAKING A STORYTELLING APPROACH TO BOARD PRESENTATIONS

Your board slides need to be more than numbers; they're about a story, including your organization's impact that you're making and will make.

Startup marketing executive Anthony Kennada says that every board slide should have a narrative that clearly explains what the person reading it should get out of it. Instead of "Marketing updates" write "We've scaled our inbound pipeline by 4X this quarter, with plans to double momentum in H2."

"Assume you're not in the room presenting; can someone still get what you're hoping for them to get out of the slide?" says Kennada.

Be honest with the board, including about past performance, and be clear about learnings. Build a strong relationship with your CFO (or CEO if they're doing the finance). Find out what metrics are important to the board and adapt your language to make it easy for anyone outside the day-to-day business to understand.

COMMUNICATE WITH YOUR DEPARTMENT TEAM TO GET WHAT YOU NEED FROM THEM

You'll need to report on metrics and talk about business performance at a high level. Give your team within your department plenty of time to prepare any materials you'll be referencing on their behalf, such as results metrics, funnel metrics, etc. We've all been there when the boss asks us to send materials last-minute because they procrastinated on their board slides! (Try not to do this.) It's great to share with your team what you're able to after the board meeting to help everyone understand on another level how their work is tied to the business goals.

CREATING YOUR BOARD SLIDES: THINK AT A HIGH ALTITUDE

The board wants to know what you've learned, and how you're applying that knowledge to drive key business growth—namely revenue growth and retention. Beyond the tactical, how can you share at a high level which programs you've invested in and how you've applied data and resources to be successful?

Things boards want to know:

- What is the status of progress in your department and how should they be thinking about the performance/metrics as they relate to the overall business growth? What's the analysis of the data and why are the numbers where they are?
- What have you learned since the last board meeting? How have you applied what you've learned to improve (or will you apply them?)
- What's a risk in your department and how will you meet the challenge?
- What programs are you planning for the next quarter, half, and/or year, and what do you expect the impact will be on the business growth? How will you get to the goals and what assumptions/data are you incorporating in your program?

HOW TO CREATE YOUR BOARD SLIDES

Many new executives struggle with board presentations due to inexperience and improper preparation. To be effective, you need to understand the specific things the board is looking for in presentations.

"For many executives, they present to the board, the board says nice things and then when the executive leaves, the board thinks, 'that was kind of a waste of time.' Hence, these executives are considered to be 'not strategic'," says Gainsight CEO Nick Mehta.

This can be mitigated by focusing on the right things and preparing a presentation that will effectively communicate your impact and learnings to the board. To deliver a strong board presentation, Mehta suggests the following:

- Whenever including metrics, also include a plan for improving it. Without associating it with a goal and/or plan can leave the board wondering how to interpret it.
- Whenever including a metric, show how the metric has trended over time.
- Color code your metrics (red/yellow/green) to make them easier to read and understand.

- Don't use acronyms that will confuse the board (e.g., internal acronyms that they're not up-to-speed on and/or jargon that isn't common in business parlance, like PQL/SQL/ABM, without explaining).
- Ensure metrics being shown (e.g., growth, adoption, signups) tie back to the areas the board most cares about, like revenue, retention, and/or LTV.
- Make the slide title the headline story ("revenue is up 50% YoY" vs. "revenue"). Make it as easy as possible for the board to understand your intended narrative.
- When including charts and/or visuals, include a text box next to it with key takeaways, and highlight key data points and label them. You want any visuals to tell a clear story and for it to be as easy as possible for your board to interpret the results. (Note: Wiley book *Storytelling with Data* by Cole Knaflic is a fantastic resource for learning how to improve your data visualization skills!)

EXAMPLE DEPARTMENT OKR SNAPSHOT SLIDE REPORTING RESULTS WITH R/Y/G

Best quarter ever in top- and mid-funnel performance (2x target), setting up a strong H1 as the sales team scales.

OKR	KPI	R/Y/G
Opportunity Generation	100 new Marketing Qualified Opportunities (MQOs) for Enterprise Deals in Q1	95 MQOs Forecast: 98 MQOs by end of Q1
Increase engagement inside target accounts	2,000 new MQLs by End of Q1	2,300 MQLS
Deliver high ROI content and activate growth channels	30 new content pieces (2 pillar, 13 medium and small) shipped by End of Q1; Activating 2 new growth channels (Video, Events)	35+ content pieces delivered (4 pillar, 12 podcasts 25 blogs, 2 case studies; Activating 2 new growth channels (Video, Events)

OTHER TYPES OF SLIDES TO INCLUDE IN YOUR BOARD DECK

- **Title slide** (your department, your name, include the company logo—use the slide template your company provides, if possible).
- **An OKR slide** (example above).
- **A slide showing metrics trending over time with % change and explanations in call-out boxes** (e.g., marketing funnel performance quarter-to-date QTD compared to previous QTD and year-over-year trends).
- **Narrative-driven slide highlighting the programs and initiatives you've built and how they are tied to the results you achieved in the last period** (e.g., "Taking our brand mainstream by converting thought leadership into revenue to drive 150% increase in marketing pipeline or 3X growth year-over-year" with examples of the new channels and campaigns you ran that led to the results you showed in the prior slide, or in the appendix").
- **Narrative-driven slide highlighting what you've learned from the quarter or half, and opportunities you see for applying those insights** (e.g., "We learned that ABM is the path to scaling demand generation within our target accounts and are doubling down on our account-based programs next quarter").
- **Appendix** (title slide to demarcate that all subsequent slides should be viewed as additional reference material and not part of your live presentation).
- **Appendix** (slides) (these slides show additional details that the board can dig into if they choose, with granularity in areas you've covered at a high level earlier in the presentation).

THE PURPOSE OF YOUR APPENDIX AND/OR PRE-READ MATERIAL

Appendix slides or separate materials you send to your CEO to share with the board before the meeting (often called a "pre-read") may include detail on tactical programs and campaigns that roll up to the major themes or points you cover in the presentation, references into processes, and department organization structure. For example, you might include a team slide with everyone's title and face on your team and/or showing the organization hiring plan and dates you expect to fill roles. Don't expect to review an appendix or additional pre-read material during the board meeting. It's great to include more materials in the deck that the board can choose to review if they want more details about your program.

For example, in marketing, an appendix slide could show the "science" of marketing and how we measure lead scoring and what our funnel looks like as we build awareness and generate leads and opportunities that become validated by sales. The board doesn't need to see these during the presentation—that level of detail isn't part of the conversation at that stage—but if they have questions, it's helpful for them to get to see the thought and strategy behind the high-level overview.

Other examples of slides you could include in the appendix:

- Team organization structure/hiring plan.
- More details on the programs you launched that quarter and their performance relative to previous quarters.
- Initiatives you plan to run in the future/following quarters—the preview of what you'll be talking about in the next board meeting.
- A slide showing your revenue funnel and/or expansion motion.
- Your sales process.

Note: board members will often read highly detailed slides, including the appendix, ahead of time so you don't need to spend time reviewing that level of detail during the meeting.

TIP: ENSURE EVERY SLIDE HAS A NARRATIVE-DRIVEN TITLE

Every slide should tell a story that your board can understand quickly without digging into the entire slide. Here are some examples for how to turn each slide into a narrative-driven format:

Weak: Q3 OKRs

Better: best half ever for opportunity generation setting up a strong H2 as AEs Ramp.

Weak: Q3 Metrics (Continued)

Better: our performance in H1 was 3X stronger YoY, setting the stage for a strong H2.

Weak: H1 Learning

Better: we learned key insights in H1 that will enable us to scale our growth engine in H2.

Weak: H2 goals

Better: we are committing to generating 300 opportunities in H2 to nearly double our momentum this year.

PRESENTATION TIPS: BEFORE, DURING, AND AFTER THE BOARD MEETING

Before the Meeting

Show your slides to your CEO and/or a friendly board member to get their feedback. Plan to review them together to talk through questions that the board may have, make sure your slides clearly communicate the story of your results and learnings, as well as your plans as they align to the overall business growth goals.

Remember that your board is there because they want you and your company to succeed. If you're going to be the one presenting, and you have a meditation and/or other mindfulness practice, it's helpful to do that before a board meeting. If you can, try to clear your schedule right before the board meeting to give yourself extra time to "get in the game." Prepare a run-through of your slides if possible.

Practice Helps You Succeed

If you can, build a relationship with at least one board member and share your slides with them in advance (with the CEO's blessing).

"Use that as a dress rehearsal, for your presentation and say, 'here's what I'm hoping to communicate to the board. Here's what I'm hoping to get from the board. Here's what I'm hoping will be the inputs and feedback and support from the board in these areas'," says Matt Heinz.

Sharing with someone friendly on the board or your CEO prior to the meeting can be crucial for assessing your blind spots and ensuring you're putting together the most impactful board decks.

During the Meeting

The board meeting itself may or may not include you; in many early-stage start-ups, you'll send your board materials to your CEO, and they will present them on your behalf. If you're going to present in-person and/or on a conference call to the board, you'll need to prepare yourself mentally in addition to the slides. Sometimes you'll be invited to jump into the meeting and/or on Zoom for a portion of the board call.

While presenting, try to relax and embrace humble confidence as you demonstrate that you're thinking strategically about the areas you own, while being open to learning and adapting so you're constantly iterating on plans to improve each KPI that the board cares about (e.g., revenue, retention, increased LTV).

As you present, try to relax and speak slowly. If you're asked a question you don't know the answer to, say so and get back to the board after (follow up with your CEO for best practice on this). Focus on what you've prepared in your slides, and be willing to take note of any board questions that you don't know the answer to and commit to getting back to them (and then do this).

After the Board Meeting

After checking with your CEO, send the board any materials they requested that you didn't have on hand at the time. For example, if they wanted to see a three-week growth period, you needed to pull the metrics. Answer any lingering questions, and/or send a thank you to the board for their time. After the meeting, try to get feedback from your CEO and/or that friendly board member with whom you've built a relationship to find out what you did well and what you can improve for next time. If you're open to growth and learning, you'll be an asset to your CEO and to your company and they'll be proud to put you in front of board members. Plus, who knows? Those board members may be on your board at the next company you join, so it can help to create long-term relationships. (VCs are in it for the long game.)

CHAPTER TWENTY

Mentorship: How to Further Grow Your Career by Networking and Giving Back

No executive goes it alone. You may be a first-time executive, but you have a lot to offer (and gain) from sharing with your peer network, team, and startup community.

When I became a mentor at Techstars, a leading accelerator with a presence around the world, I learned its manifesto "give first," which means to give without an expectation of receiving (knowing we mentors will still likely receive a lot from the experience). I didn't realize how important this was to my startup philosophy until I encountered ecosystems where that mentality wasn't the case. It made me understand that generosity without expectation is truly the lifeblood of a successful startup ecosystem. There is so much to learn and limited resources to accomplish a startup's mission and goals.

MENTORSHIP POWERS THE STARTUP ECOSYSTEM

I know what mentorship means both to myself as a mentor and to the founders with whom I have had the privilege of interacting. Techstars says that mentor relationships almost always become two-way. That's definitely been true for me as I have been a lead mentor in Sustainability and Workforce Development accelerators and with Backstage Capital.

One founder I mentored invited me to his baby shower two years after our mentorship relationship officially ended, and we regularly talk about life, relationships, as well as the startup world. Plus, we now send each other original songs about startup life. (Ditto to another Techstars alum and co-founder I mentored. What is it about music as a way to ease the pressure of the startup world?) Another mentor and I have a more formal relationship, but we have stayed in touch long after his program ended, and I consider all three of these founders as friends. They've helped me with life topics as much as I've helped their companies with their go-to-market strategies. That's the gift of mentoring; whether you're aiming to give or receive, know that it'll be something that goes both ways.

MENTORSHIP'S ROLE IN SUPPORTING DEVELOPING LEADERS

Sales leader Mary Carter leads a high-performing sales team at GoCardless and provides mentorship to many in the industry. She mentors others now, and credits the mentors who helped her with providing advice not only on how to succeed in her role and get promoted but how to balance the demands of work with peace of mind and a sense of home-life equilibrium.

"I was lucky enough to have a really awesome mentor who taught me the foundations of professionalism and the lay of the land of tech, applications, and players, but also personal advice," says Carter.

MENTORSHIP IS ABOUT KNOWLEDGE AND CHEMISTRY

Mergelane co-founder Sue Heilbronner says a good mentor–mentee relationship needs personal connection and chemistry.

"Once you get through specific content and facts like 'this person has great experience in finance' and 'this person could use some bolstering in their knowledge in this area,' the connection is the thing," says Heilbronner.

"Mentees are most successful when they think about identifying mentors as people who are already in their world with whom they have a big connection; it's true for mentors also. We have formal structures in accelerators, incubators, and that's all fantastic as a way to facilitate and enhance the power of mentorship, but informal opportunities can be very meaningful."

MENTORS DON'T HAVE TO KNOW ALL OF THE ANSWERS

I've learned as a mentor to ask good questions and be open to how the recipient wants to navigate their answers, releasing ideas of how I think they "should" handle a situation, and trusting them to be the best judge of their own course of action. Mentors can advise and provide guidance but don't oversteer. There's great power in also knowing that when I receive mentorship, I can choose to listen to what resonates and discard the rest.

For example, I once was talking to a founder about a challenge with one of his co-founders around their average sales price (ASP) and how he was feeling about their difference of opinion. I didn't try to tell him what to do or even push him to decide what action to take. I had my own opinion about what ASP would work best for their target market, but that wasn't what he needed. Instead of pushing an agenda, I was there to listen to what he wanted to share on the topic and come to his own answers.

He ended up solving his problem by engaging a coach to facilitate some difficult conversations with him and his co-founder about their company vision and how they wanted to go to market. He found our chats helpful to clarify his own needs and thinking. I'm proud that they took these insights into their next successful fundraising event, now on the same page about the *why* behind their pricing strategy.

ENLISTING YOUR OWN MENTORS: DEVELOPING A GROUP OF PERSONAL ADVISORS

To get a diverse perspective on your startup role, build relationships with advisors who can serve as a kind of personal board. These folks bring subject matter expertise, leadership experience, as well as motivational support.

These are a few roles to consider recruiting to your personal advisory board:

- Peers (around the same career tenure). Share common stories and comradery. I call up friends who are dealing with the same issues and we help each other navigate success.
- Someone five to ten years more experienced than you are. This may be a peer, but ideally someone who has been there and can reflect back on what you're going through now without being too far removed.

- A Board member. Either from your board or someone who sits on a board and can teach you how boards think.
- A domain knowledge expert. Someone who knows your domain well, or perhaps an area you're weaker in (e.g., accounting if you're in People Ops and don't have that background).
- An executive coach. Someone who can coach you on specific leadership areas and is motivated to help you grow.
- Mentors for a specific area or your business.
- Industry analyst. Someone with industry domain experience (e.g., cloud, FinTech).

MENTORS CARE ABOUT YOU PERSONALLY AND CAN KEEP YOUR PRIORITIES STRAIGHT

Startup sales leader Mary Carter's mentor reminded her to take care of her personal needs in addition to those of her role.

"He said, insurance is a vital part of what you get with your job. What if you get hurt or sick, you need to fall back. The quicker you get this done, the quicker the administration work is out of your way and you can focus on other things. It taught me to prioritize health over work. Work is always going to be there."

Carter says now, as a leader who oversees the growth of others on her team, she tells her reports to put wellness and family first.

"That's not always a popular opinion," says Carter. "It's in our culture and society to work until you're exhausted and tired. Always being busy. But for me, if you really want to have longevity in your life, you have to enjoy what you do. You can only enjoy yourself when basic needs have been met. Prioritizing those things first. If you're sick, take a day off. If you're stressed, take a mental health day. That's the motto I've been living by. If you're with a good company, they'll support you. Some companies aren't that flexible. That may be a company someone wants to work for."

Carter encourages aspiring startup leaders to champion their growth and proactively seek help from their mentors.

"I was dedicated to upward movement, and I worked hard for it," says Carter. "As a woman of color in startups, I am proud to be paid what my work is worth, and it hasn't always been easy."

Before her first startup leadership role, Carter spent her time, in her words, "grinding," sometimes doing many sales calls per day, including technical demos, technical QA, legal calls, and working very long hours to close International deals.

"What that meant for me was yes, I was tired, yes, I had to say no to parties or friends or vacations, but it got me a title change, and it got me three promotions. You have to prove you're worth it. You have to show and quantify the work you've done in dollars, and that's not arguable," says Carter.

Mentors can also push you to "go for it" when you may not see that opportunity for yourself right away. This was also the case for Carter, who has been rapidly promoted multiple times, often preceded by the gentle push of her mentor to put her hat in the ring for new opportunities.

"My mentors have often seen things in me that tell them I'm ready before I have seen it myself, and then it's my job to go make it a reality," says Carter.

SEEK MENTORSHIP THAT PROMOTES EQUALITY

Trier Bryant is co-founder and CEO of Just Work, a strategic executive leader with distinctive tech, Wall Street, and military experience spanning over 15 years. She's previously held leadership roles at Astra, Twitter, Goldman Sachs, and served as a combat veteran in the United States Air Force as a Captain leading engineering teams while spearheading diversity, equity, and inclusion (DEI) initiatives for the Air Force Academy, Air Force, and the department of defense. She says that as a Black woman, finding mentors who "guide her the same as a white man" is important.

"When I was in the military, a white man general told me he was going to mentor me 'as if I was a white man,' because he told me 'that's who you have to compete with.' Oftentimes, people will filter their mentorship, guidance, and sponsorship through their own biased lens," says Bryant.

SIGN UP TO MENTOR AT AN ACCELERATOR

I've learned so much from mentoring at Techstars and Backstage Capital accelerator and deeply value those relationships. I proudly use my swag from their organizations and refer other mentors regularly who could be a good fit for the programs. If you want to get involved with mentoring in a more formal way, offering your departmental expertise and/or industry expertise to founders at an accelerator is a great tool. You also get to see what it's really like to be an early-stage founder in case that's something you'd like to do. I think this is also a great way to disqualify the role; you see how much pressure founders are under when you're meeting with them regularly outside of the company, without any need to appear to "have it together."

At Techstars, we first meet the founders of each cohort and hear their pitches in what's called "Mentor Madness." It's basically a half-day of hearing back-to-back 10-minute pitches where you get to see if you both have chemistry. Whether in-person or virtual, I always end the day exhausted, because I'm an introvert, and it requires being "on" with a lot of new people in one day. Yet it's satisfying to get to help early stage founders and companies find their way.

I mentor at Sustainability and Workforce Development accelerators at Techstars, two areas I have a passion for. There are now many accelerators around the world that specialize in different things and markets. Chances are, there's an accelerator near you that includes companies tackling something you care about and can provide value to. It's worth a shot if you feel it would be fulfilling.

MENTOR THROUGH AN OFFICIAL ORGANIZATION

Mentor Spaces founder Chris Motley believes in mentorship's power to transform lives. Through his platform, professionals from underrepresented backgrounds can support others and get support for their own career growth. Motley's organization works with the National Black MBA Association (NBMBAA) and other organizations. Other organizations to consider becoming a mentor at include Lesbians Who Tech, Girls Who Code, and other affinity groups.

FIND COMMUNITY AND SHARE MUTUAL SUPPORT AS A "PEER MENTOR"

Nicole Wojno Smith says finding peers and building a supportive community around you is paramount to finding and succeeding in an executive role.

"The biggest thing that I've found is that it's lonely," says Smith. "Most of the time, your CEO expects you to know how to do the job. You can't really go to them and say, hey, I really don't know how to do this. When you were director, you had your VP to ask these questions or you might have had three other peers on the same level that you could just chat with about some of this. It's kind of like overnight some of that goes away," says Smith.

Smith is a member of Pavilion, a membership-based organization that provides peer mentorship to revenue leaders at tech companies.

"You have to build your board of advisors or Executive Board of Who You Can Count On," says Wonjo Smith.

Smith asks her global group of CMO peers how to handle situations, sending them messages when in doubt (and fielding them from others). When she owned a new function within marketing recently, she turned to this group for counsel, and they are always willing to get on calls or answer messages to help her succeed.

AFFINITY ORGANIZATIONS

Having people whom you can trust to turn to outside of your company when you don't know something or just need support is crucial, especially if you're a member of an under-represented minority. Groups like People of Color in Tech, Lesbians Who Tech, or other affinity groups can help you find like-minded peers and mentors with whom you can draw and give support. Scale-up startups often have organizations like Employee Resource Groups (ERGs) around identities like LGBTQ+, Latinx, Black in Tech, Women in Tech, and more that you can join and be a part of.

OTHER TYPES OF SUPPORT: SPONSORSHIP AND COACHING

Sponsorship

A sponsor is willing to take a risk and bet on you. Sponsors are vested in your success, and often expect some kind of mutual outcome, unlike a mentor, who ideally will benefit from your interaction as well but doesn't expect to.

According to marketing executive Rachel Beisel, "I would be willing to risk my reputation to help the person throughout their career, which is more than a mentor, who may support you but isn't willing to put their reputation on the line. They know that the person they are sponsoring will make them look good and they will get something in return down the road as well. That person you sponsor encourages you to take risks and has your back. They also deliver critical feedback. They expect performance, loyalty, and advice down the road."

Coaching

Coaching tends to focus on a specific area (although not always). A coach tends to be on the sidelines, offering advice without being in the game with you (as a sponsor might be). For example, getting an executive coach or a functional area expertise coach, you'd most often pay that person to help you excel in a particular area.

DON'T DISCOUNT INFORMAL MENTORSHIP

According to Rand Fishkin, "I think a lot of people hear the word mentorship and they think I will find a mentor and we will get on the phone every week or two weeks or month or something and have an hour or 90-minute phone call and they will sort of be like a therapist-type person. That's fine. But you can also be an ally or friend to someone and mentor them informally while spending time together, and that's great too."

I have so many informal mentorship relationships, I've lost count. I think everyone in the startup world can be an ally to me, and me to them, if we're willing and have time. I especially appreciate informal mentorship in the form of friends in the startup world who share their stories, including triumphs and setbacks, because it normalizes the journey we all go through. Never underestimate what you can offer someone else outside of an "official" container.

TAKE MENTORSHIP TO THE NEXT LEVEL: SCALE YOUR IMPACT

"Mentorship means having a conversation with people who have more experience, who choose to share their lived experiences to help you accomplish your goal more, effectively more efficiently," says Mentor Spaces founder and CEO Chris Motley.

Motley's perspective is that everyone is a mentor and everyone needs a mentor. His vision is to scale mentorship by creating a mentorship economy where professionals build career currency by giving mentorship, getting mentorship and growing in their careers, one conversation at a time.

Full disclosure: I was one of Motley's Lead Mentors at Techstars for his company Mentor Spaces, which means we had a *lot* of conversations about mentorship over the course of the program (and stayed in touch after). His insights about the value of scaling mentorship through educational materials contributed to my writing this book. It really does all come full circle.

AFTERWORD

Being a startup executive is challenging on many levels. From getting your first role to performing, to managing your team to dealing with your own psychology, it's a lot, even on a good day.

Even if we succeed at our roles, growing our companies and providing tangible value, few of us will see those multi-million dollar exits we dream of. We may, but these outsized outcomes are something to aspire to, not expect.

Given this, I invite us all to be motivated by the journey. The joy of meeting a delighted customer. The power of building a team that's focused on accomplishing a shared mission to disrupt a market. The fist-bumping (or covid-friendly Zoom wave) ecstasy after closing a deal many teams worked hard on across different teams.

Then there is the heartbreak when something doesn't go your way or a market shifts out of your favor. And everything in between. The startup world is a wild ride filled with twists and turns. Plus, the regular old world is more complicated than ever, with uncertainties and challenges for so many. Attuned, authentic, and compassionate leadership is more sought after than ever in today's post-pandemic climate.

If you want to be a startup leader, you can do it. I'll be rooting for you. See you along the journey upwards!

NOTES

INTRODUCTION

1. Silicon Valley Bank (n.d.), "Half of Startups Have No Women on Their Leadership Team." Sil Retrieved October 5, 2021, from: https://www.svb.com/trends-insights/reports/women-in-technology-2019#:~:text=Just%2056%20percent%20of%20startups,the%20UK%2C%20China%20and%20Canada.
2. Tedrick, S. (2020), *Women of Color in Tech: A Blueprint for Inspiring and Mentoring the Next Generation of Technology Innovators.* John Wiley & Sons, Inc., p. viii.
3. Ibid.
4. "Women in IT: Five Strategies for Making it to the Top," Deloitte United States, August 2, 2018. Retrieved October 5, 2021, from: https://www2.deloitte.com/us/en/pages/technology-media-and-telecommunications/articles/women-in-it.html.
5. CompTIA (n.d.). *2020 IT* "Information Technology) Industry Trends Analysis: Business of Technology: Comptia." Retrieved October 5, 2021, from: https://www.comptia.org/content/research/it-industry-outlook-2020#:~:text=Industry%20Overview,to%20the%20research%20consultancy%20IDC.
6. Mendoza, N. F. (2020, April 21), "US Tech Industry Had 12.1 Million Employees in 2019," *TechRepublic.* Retrieved November 6, 2021, from: https://www.techrepublic.com/article/us-tech-industry-had-12-1-million-employees-in-2019/.
7. Statista Research Department (2021, January 20), "New Entrepreneurial Businesses U.S. 2020. *Statista.* Retrieved November 6, 2021, from: https://www.statista.com/statistics/235494/new-entrepreneurial-businesses-in-the-us/.
8. Written by Chris Orlob, who is a Director of Sales at Gong.io. (2019, January 17). "The VP Sales' Average Tenure Shrank in 7 Months—Here's Why. Gong." Retrieved November 6, 2021, from: https://www.gong.io/blog/vp-sales-average-tenure/

CHAPTER ONE

1. Azoulay, P., Jones, B. F., Miranda, J., and Kim, J. D. K. (2021, January 20). "Research: The Average Age of a Successful Startup Founder is 45," *Harvard Business Review*. Retrieved November 4, 2021, from: https://hbr.org/2018/07/research-the-average-age -of-a-successful-startup-founder-is-45.
2. "Why Women Don't Apply for Jobs Unless They're 100% Qualified," *Harvard Business Review* (2021, November 2). Retrieved November 6, 2021, from: https://hbr.org/2014/08 /why-women-dont-apply-for-jobs-unless-theyre-100-qualified.
3. Scott, K. I. M. (2021). *Just Work: Get Sh*t Done, Fast and Fair. Essay*, Macmillan, p. 195.
4. "How Apple Is Organized for Innovation," *Harvard Business Review* (2021, August 27). Retrieved November 6, 2021, from: https://hbr.org/2020/11/how-apple-is-organized -for-innovation.

CHAPTER TWO

1. Mochary, M., MacCaw, A., and Talavera, M. (2019), *The Great CEO Within: A Tactical Guide to Company Building*, Matt Mochary, p. 108.

CHAPTER THREE

1. Esther Perel on Scott Galoway podcast Prof. G. Show, "Eros, Self-Awareness, and Being a Good Partner" (2021, April 8). Prof. G. Show, episode.
2. Bussgang, J. (2017), *Entering Startupland: An Essential Guide to Finding the Right Job*, Harvard Business School Press, p. 10. Retrieved from: https://store.hbr.org/product /entering-atartupland-an-essential-guide-to-finding-the-right-job/10162?sku=10162 E-KND-ENG.
3. Gender Equity Gap Study: "Analysis. Table Stakes" (2020, December 9). Retrieved November 6, 2021, from: https://tablestakes.com/study-2019/.

CHAPTER FIVE

1. Carter, A. (2022), *Ask for More: 10 Questions to Negotiate Anything*, Simon & Schuster, pp. 46–67.
2. Ibid.
3. Ibid.

4. Kuper, S. (2019), *Secrets of Sand Hill Road: Venture Capital-And How To Get It*, Virgin Books, p.185.
5. Constine, J. (2018, September 18), "The Gap Table: Women Own Just 9% of Startup Equity," *TechCrunch*. Retrieved November 6, 2021, from: https://techcrunch.com /2018/09/18/the-gap-table/.

CHAPTER SIX

1. Jack Altman, *People Strategy*, p. 49.

CHAPTER SEVEN

1. Scott, K. (2021), *Just Work: Get Sh*t Done, Fast and Fair*, Macmillon, p. 32.

CHAPTER EIGHT

1. Elid Gil, *High Growth Handbook*, p. 199.
2. Joy, M. (2020), *The Vegan Matrix: Understanding and Discussing Privilege Among Vegans to Build a More Inclusive and Empowered Movement*, Lantern Publishing and Media, pp. 20–22.
3. Ibid.
4. Harts, M. (2020). *The Memo: What Women of Color Need to Know to Secure a Seat at the Table*, Seal Press, p. 157.
5. Tedrick, S. (2020), *Women of Color in Tech: A Blueprint for Inspiring and Mentoring the Next Generation of Technology Innovators*, John Wiley & Sons, Inc.

CHAPTER NINE

1. "Millennials Want Business to Shift Its Purpose," Deloitte United States (2020, April 24). Retrieved November 6, 2021, from: https://www2.deloitte.com/us/en/pages/about -deloitte/articles/millennials-shifting-business-purpose.html.
2. Blanche, A. (2017, April 5), "Tech Firms Striving for Diversity Fixate on the Wrong Metric. Wired." Retrieved November 6, 2021, from: https://www.wired.com/2017/04/tech -firms-striving-diversity-fixate-wrong-metric/.

3. Hasson, G., and Butler, D. (2020), *Mental Health and Wellbeing in the Workplace: A Practical Guide for Employers and Employees*, Capstone, p. 81.
4. Esther Perel on Scott Galoway podcast Prof. G Show, "Eros, Self-Awareness, and Being a Good Partner" (2021, April 8), Prof G Show, episode.

CHAPTER TEN

1. Dixon-Fyle, S., Dolan, K., Hunt, V., and Prince, S. (2021, November 2), "Diversity Wins: How Inclusion Matters," McKinsey & Company. Retrieved November 6, 2021, from: https://www.mckinsey.com/featured-insights/diversity-and-inclusion/diversity-wins -how-inclusion-matters.
2. Hoffman, R., Yeh, C., and Casnocha, B. (2013), The Alliance: Managing Talent in the Networked Age, HarperCollins, p. 8.

CHAPTER ELEVEN

1. Scott, K. (2021), *Just Work: Get Sh*t Done, Fast and Fair*, Macmillan, p.1.
2. Ibid p. 10.

CHAPTER TWELVE

1. Frei, F., and Morriss, A. (2020), *Unleashed: The Unapologetic Leader's Guide to Empowering Everyone Around You*, Harvard Business Review Press. Retrieved from: https://store.hbr .org/product/unleashed-the-unapologetic-leader-s-guide-to-empowering-everyone -around-you/10245.

CHAPTER THIRTEEN

1. Peper, E., Harvey, R., and Faass, N. (2020), *Tech Stress: How Technology Is Hijacking Our Lives, Strategies for Coping, and Pragmatic Ergonomics*, North Atlantic Books, p. 29.
2. Fairchild, C. (2021, June 3), "The Office Didn't Work for Most Black Employees. Here's How We Can Change That as They Reopen," LinkedIn. Retrieved November 6, 2021, from: https://www.linkedin.com/pulse/office-didnt-work-most-black-employees-heres -how-we-can-fairchild/?trackingId=s%2FSjGYuL0LJP9SnvE11EFg%3D%3D.

3. Fosslien, L., and Duffy, M. W. (2019), *No Hard Feelings: The Secret Power of Embracing Emotions at Work*, Portfolio/Penguin, an imprint of Penguin Random House LLC, p. 208.
4. Brown, J. (2021), *How To Be an Inclusive Leader: Your Role in Creating Cultures of Belonging Where Everyone Can Thrive*, Berrett-Koehler, p. 84.

CHAPTER FIFTEEN

1. *Women in the Workplace* (2021), LeanIn.organization and McKinsey & Company. Retrieved November 6, 2021, from: https://womenintheworkplace.com/.
2. Ibid.
3. *A New Era of Workplace Inclusion: Moving From Retrofit to Redesign*, Future Forum (2021, March 11). Retrieved November 6, 2021, from: https://futureforum.com/2021/03/11/dismantling-the-office-moving-from-retrofit-to-redesign/.

CHAPTER SEVENTEEN

1. "Women in Tech Survey," *Capital One*. Retrieved November 6, 2021, from: https://www.capitalone.com/about/newsroom/women-in-tech-survey/.
2. Neef, K. (2022). *Fierce Self-compassion: How Women Can Harness Kindness to Speak Up, Claim Their Power, and . . . Thrive*, Penguin Life, pp. 20–22.
3. Ibid.
4. Blanche, A., "Hi. I'm Aubrey Blanche and I'm Bipolar—The Mathpath". Retrieved November 6, 2021, from: https://aubreyblanche.com/blog/hi-im-aubrey-blanche-and-im-bipolar.

ACKNOWLEDGMENTS

The not-so-well-hidden secret of business book publishing is that books require a mighty team effort. This book is born from the tremendous support, help, and guidance of numerous individuals. To the editorial and publishing sages Bill Faloon, Purvi Patel, Samantha Enders, Patricia Bateson, Abirami Srikandan, and Ashok Ravi, and the entire team at Wiley: You took a leap on me and for that I am unbelievably lucky and grateful. To Brad Feld, who introduced me to the Wiley team and has been a tremendous source of support and guidance along my startup journey. Your kindness ripples throughout many startup ecosystems, and I've been one of the many lucky ones impacted by your "give first" ethos.

To the contributors who generously shared their original insights in this book: Rachel Beisel, Chris Peacock, Allen Chong, John Rex, Aubrey Blanche, Anne Morriss, Chris Senesi, Gerry Valentine, Nick Mehta, Sue Heilbronner, Samantha McKenna, Mindy Lauck, Erin Rand, Emilia D'Anzica, Kaley Klemp, Jennifer Rice, Evan Hung, Jeff Bussgang, Analiese Brown, Nicole Wojno Smith, Jeff Ammons, Matt Heinz, Chris Motley, Dennis Adsit, Stephon Striplin, Matt Harada, Rand Fishkin, Jerry Colonna, Sarah Innocenzi, Colleen Blake, April Wensel, Dave King, Alana Corbett, Katrin Grunwald, Julie Penner, Kalev Kaarna, Dave Cass, Therese Pcornick, Nils Vinje, Josh Ashton, Hiten Shah, Taylor McLemore, Anthony Kennada, Mary Carter, Trier Bryant, and Kate Ghidinelli. Your contributions added invaluable advice and wisdom.

To my book coach, Anne Janzer, thank you for being the greatest fairy book godmother an author could ask for. To early readers, Stephon Striplin and Matt Harada: I am deeply grateful for your tremendous feedback. This book is so much better because of you.

Thank you to supporters Arlan Hamilton, Carly Brantz, Nicolle Paradise, Rob Castaneda, Samuel Hulick, Michael Pollack, Fima Leshinsky, Bill Cushard, Marjorie Abdelkrime, Sven Lackinger, Maximilian Messing, Eliot Peper, Erik Grand, Daniel Luebke, Colleen Trinkaus, Lindsay Crafford, and Tony Faccenda.

Another note of gratitude to my dear family and friends. You're the reason I do the things I do. I love you! Finally, to my former, current, and future colleagues, and everyone in the startup ecosystem who's ever wondered if they had what it takes to lead: I'm so lucky to get to be on this journey with you. Here's to leading upwards together!

ABOUT
THE AUTHOR

Sarah E. Brown is a B2B tech marketing leader, author, startup mentor, and ecosystem builder with more than a decade of experience scaling SaaS companies through customer-centric marketing. She has been a marketing leader at five startups that have been sold for more than $300 million combined. She is a mentor at Techstars and Backstage Capital accelerators, the founder of Flatirons Tech, an LGBTQ+ tech group based in Boulder, CO, and co-organizer of SF Bay Area Vegans in Tech.

INDEX